YORKSHIRE

At War

A nostalgic look back at momentous events through personal memories

RON FREETHY

Dalesman

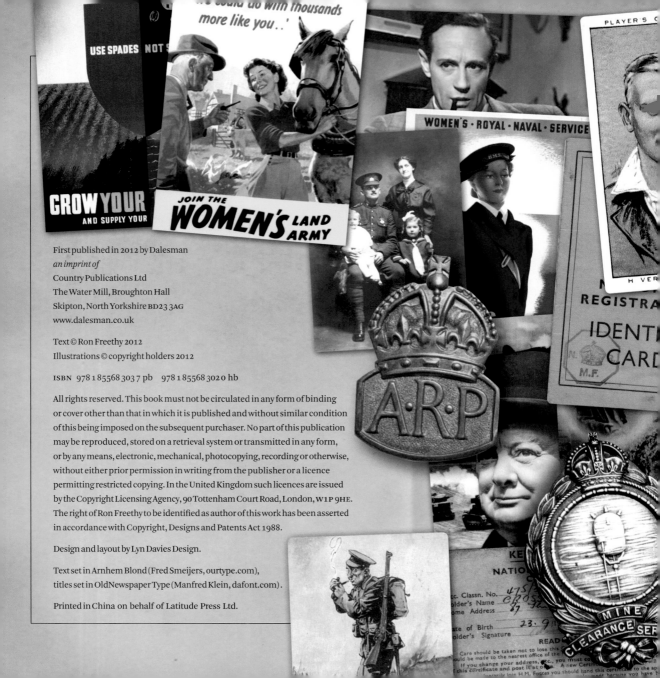

First published in 2012 by Dalesman
an imprint of
Country Publications Ltd
The Water Mill, Broughton Hall
Skipton, North Yorkshire BD23 3AG
www.dalesman.co.uk

ISBN   978 1 85568 303 7 pb   978 1 85568 302 0 hb

Design and layout by Lyn Davies Design.

Text set in Arnhem Blond (Fred Smeijers, ourtype.com),
titles set in OldNewspaper Type (Manfred Klein, dafont.com).

Printed in China on behalf of Latitude Press Ltd.

CONTENTS

INTRODUCTION

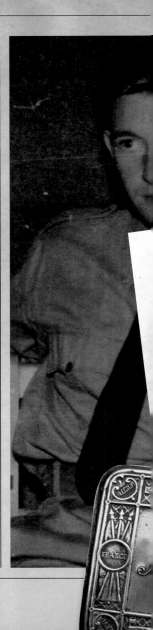

WHEN I WAS FIRST ASKED to take this nostalgic look back at Yorkshire at War I did not think that, with the focus firmly fixed upon photographs and images, it would be easy. How wrong I was. My brief was to concentrate on events between 1900 and 1960, and I was lucky to be old enough to have clear memories of the Second World War. I was also lucky in that my wife had a collection of memories from family members relating to the First World War.

What did surprise me was the number of images dating back even to the Boer War and an event now called the Russian Outrage, which almost resulted in a war with Russia in the days of the Tsar and long before the Russian Revolution.

I was able to trawl newspaper archives and especially through the back numbers of *Down Your Way* and *Dalesman* magazines. The result has been a record of Yorkshire's part in war in a few words and lots of pictures.

I hope that it will inspire people to write down and collect any family pictures which they may have tucked away in an attic. My request for memories of National Service, which was essential following the Second World War, resulted in such a flood of material that it could well have resulted in a book of its own.

This book proves beyond any doubt that Yorkshire played a major role in keeping the peace in our land.

RON FREETHY 2012

AUTHOR'S NOTE

During the preparation of this book I have been given both help and encouragement from many friends and family. I do, however, owe a debt of gratitude to the contributors to *Dalesman* and especially the *Down Your Way* magazines, who are mentioned in the text by name or acknowledged on page 124. To my wife Marlene I am grateful for her memories, but also for her skill and patience in converting my notorious handwriting into 'computer-speak'. To Keith Hall I am appreciative for the use of his collection of images and for his untiring efforts in locating essential images.

Producing a manuscript is only part of the process, and I am grateful for the editor and design staff at Dalesman Publishing whose skills have resulted in the attractive book with which I am very proud to have been associated.

MBER SCARBOROUGH!

THE KING AT THE FRONT. The King meets a hospital matron

THE FIRST WORLD WAR

THE GIRLS ARE SIMPLY FIGHTING FOR ME.

AE

The Dogger Bank incident

When we look at Yorkshire today, especially with regard to its coastal holiday resorts, it is hard to imagine a time when the whole county was engaged in waging two world wars and almost three.

Few realise that in 1904 and 1905 Britain almost went to war with Tsarist Russia as a result of a catastrophic error. The event has become known as the Dogger Bank Incident but also as the Russian Outrage.

It all started on 21st October 1904 when the *Gamecock* fleet of forty trawlers set out from Hull to fish the Dogger Bank grounds which are some 200 miles (320km) off Spurn Head. At this time the Russians were at war with the Japanese, and the Tsar's armament in his Baltic Fleet included seven battleships, six cruisers and a number of fast torpedo boats. The group was on its way to their rendezvous at Port Arthur in the Far East when they sighted the Hull fishing trawlers. These were mistaken for Japanese torpedo boats, and so the Russians turned on their searchlights and opened fire.

The trawler *Crane* took the brunt of the onslaught; skipper George Smith and third hand William Leggitt were killed instantly, and several others were badly injured. It was obvious that the *Crane* was sinking and her shattered crew were taken aboard the *Gull* even though this vessel herself was badly damaged. The vessels *Mino* and *Moulmein* also suffered some superficial damage. By this time the Russians had realised their mistake but, instead of giving aid to the trawlers, they sailed away, which obviously added to the anger of the people of Hull.

The whole incident obviously became a dangerous flashpoint, which was only defused when the Tsar and King Edward VII reached an agreement. The officers of the warships were to be court-martialled and they would also pay £65,000 in compensation. In the event none of this happened because the Japanese fleet destroyed the Russians during the Battle of Tsu-Shima early in 1905.

There is a memorial to the victims of the Russian outrage on the Boulevard at Hull (below left) and among the artefacts in the City Museum are some items from the trawler *Mino* damaged by the Russian shells.

At that time the men of Hull were still fighting for their lives in the Boer Wars between 1902–4. There is an impressive soldiers' memorial in the city. This is known as the South African War memorial.

opposite *Crew of the* Mino *standing next to the damage inflicted by the Russian Baltic Fleet*

right *The memorial on the Boulevard in Hull in memory of the sailors who died in the Russian Outrage*

The Scarborough Blitz

When we think of the word 'Blitz' we think of the Second World War and of London, Sheffield, Coventry, Leeds, Liverpool, Manchester and Hull – all cities devastated by raiders from the air.

In the First World War, however, Scarborough had to endure its own Blitz – which came not from the air but from the sea. When war broke out in 1914 the Kaiser's navy was determined to compete with the British Fleet; they knew how important it was to strike the first blow. In December 1914 three warships weighed anchor and had a clear battle plan in mind. They would bombard the Yorkshire coast and also lay a good number of mines in the British shipping lanes. Their aim was also to attack the developing naval wireless stations operating along the Yorkshire coastline.

The Germans sent their best vessels, led by the battleship *Derrflinger* which was 689 feet (210m) long, had a crew of 1,100, and was bristling with powerful guns and a stock of torpedoes. She was supported

REMEMBER SCARBOROUGH

ENLIST NOW

opposite left Damage to a Scarborough boarding house

opposite right A huge shell went right through the middle of Scarborough lighthouse, leaving it uninhabitable

above Bomb damage to Merryweather's food store

by the *Van Der Tann* which was almost the same size, and she was backed up by the light cruiser *Kolberg* whose function was to lay mines.

The bombardment began at 8.05am on a misty morning of 16th December 1914. The attack was both well organised, accurately aimed and had a devastating effect.

At first the local people thought it was a thunderstorm but they soon realised that this was war as houses began to fall down

at the end of the engagement. The town was soon blanketed in a pall of brown smoke. Eighteen people were killed and eighty-four others were injured. It is perhaps surprising that there was not more devastation as 519 German shells fell on the town.

Many buildings were damaged including the town hall, the Grand Hotel and the Spa. The lighthouse was badly damaged and was not fully operational again until 1931.

The authorities were quick to react, and recruitment posters were printed which read 'Remember Scarborough – ENLIST NOW'.

The German ships also shelled Whitby and Hartlepool, and certainly brought the horrors of war to the civilian population.

There were also attacks from the air by German zeppelins; on 6th June 1915 bombs were dropped on the Queen Street area of Hull and there was substantial damage.

These attacks did have an effect: there was a massive increase in men volunteering to go to war.

Trawlers join the war effort

It was not only the coastal bombardment which brought the First World War home to Yorkshire folk. The menace of minefields and U-boats meant that Hull's trawler fleet was brought into front-line action. The port had at that time the largest fishing fleet in Europe, and the trawler was the ideal vessel for both locating mines and helping in their disposal. Furthermore the crews were skilled seamen used to working under extreme weather conditions.

At first the system of minesweeping was not at all well organised but, when thirty-two Hull trawlers had been sunk by mines, the Admiralty had to act. They formed the Mine Clearance Service, and in this context 'Mad Ted' Rilatt deserves a mention. He operated his trawlers in both wars. He was not mad but just did not suffer fools gladly and thus made enemies in high places. The Admiralty's policy was to

requisition not only a trawler but also her crew, but the vessel had to be captained by a very junior royal naval officer. Many of these lads had hardly ever been to sea and 'Mad Ted' had no intention of handing his

vessel over. He was certainly hot-tempered and eccentric, but he was also unpredictable when dealing with a pompous and overbearing naval officer. Ted, however, proved to be a very able skipper and one

right Ted Rilatt; not 'Mad Ted' but a brave and efficient seaman

below U-boat U25 alongside a sinking ship, 1914–15. At this stage of the war, U-boat commanders were instructed to let crews leave their vessels before attacking with surface guns

who was very predictable when at sea and under fire. All his crews respected him and followed his orders to the letter.

Minesweeping was one problem which had to be dealt with, but another major worry was the ever-increasing menace of the U-boats. In the days when aircraft were practically non-existent, airships were used to search for the underwater menace. I spoke some years ago to Douglas Porter, who was then in his ninety-fifth year, who told me:

"I spent my life in the Merchant Navy and we all knew that being torpedoed by a U-boat was the constant danger. You could not see it until it blew your ship to hell. In 1915 we felt safer when we saw an airship overhead as it patrolled on the look-out for U-boats. I now know that they were nobbut just big bags of explosive hydrogen gas. There were lots of gas generating plants all over the country but mainly around the seaports where escorting airships were based. We thought these bags of gas and the crews which flew in them were the perfect answer to the war in the air, which was unknown at this time."

left Ted and his crew aboard the trawler Dawn celebrate their sinking of a U-boat

below A hydrogen gas generating plant

An airship pilot at his controls

The birth of war in the skies

It has always been a fault of a younger generation not to listen to their old folk and nobody knows this better than I. In 1946 when I was ten my grandfather told me that he had worked with Barnes Wallis. When I knew that he had worked on submarines at the Vickers Shipyard in Barrow-in-Furness I thought that it was just the ramblings of an old man. I should have listened to him.

Barnes Wallis, long before he became famous as the designer of the Wellington

Bomber and designed the dam-busting bomb, had indeed worked at the Vickers yards in Barrow and was a designer of airships. He had a very able assistant called Nevil Shute, who later became a famous novelist. Long after my grandfather died I found a large box in which there was a tray of drawing instruments with a name on it. This name was 'Mr Wallis'.

Much later in 1979 whilst I was working for the BBC I interviewed eighty-seven-year-old Stanley Jamieson, who told me:

"All my life I have had two main interests, which were finding out about aircraft flying at high levels and playing golf at a very low level. I was living in Otley and had the ambition to play every golf course in Yorkshire. I went to play the Spaldington course near Howden which is just off the present M62 not far from Goole. As I went round I noticed what seemed to be two very large hangers but there was no runway. I later went into the clubhouse and found lots of photographs of airships on the walls."

What happened was that Barnes Wallis and Nevil Shute had been relocated by Vickers from Barrow-in-Furness to Spaldington, and this site is now part of the golf course. It was here that the airship R100 was designed and built. How airships would have evolved if it had not been for the disaster involving the R101 in 1930 we will never know.

Actually there were two main companies competing for the dominance of the airship industry: one based at Spaldington working on the R100; and Cardington in Bedfordshire which built the R101. It was the Cardington project which failed and the R100 design performed perfectly. Despite this the British government abandoned all plans to build airships but the Germans continued to build Zeppelins well into the 1930s.

Barnes Wallis was versatile enough to turn his attention to aircraft design, and he applied his expert knowledge of light alloys and the metal strut Meccano-like design which he had already used in airships to construct his Wellington bomber. By that time, however, it was obvious that the only serious attempts to wage war in the skies would be to develop heavier-than-air and faster-moving aeroplanes.

The first fighting aircraft

When I was first married in 1962 I had just completed my RAF service, based mainly on the Island of Malta. My next-door neighbour was Billy Greenaway who was already in his nineties. In later life Billy had worked in the textile industry, but as a young man he had been in the Royal Flying Corps before it was rebranded under the name of the Royal Air Force. Billy told me:

"Not many people realise how important Yorkshire was in both world wars but also in the early history of flying. We all know

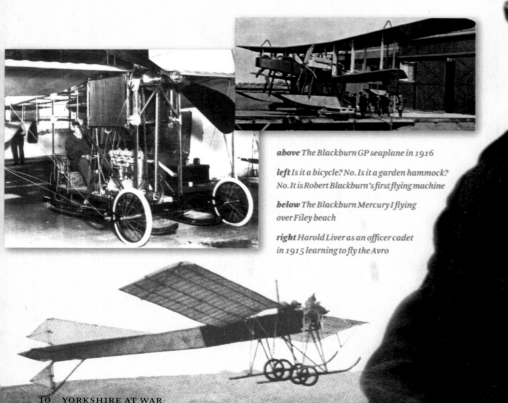

above The Blackburn GP seaplane in 1916

left Is it a bicycle? No. Is it a garden hammock? No. It is Robert Blackburn's first flying machine

below The Blackburn Mercury I flying over Filey beach

right Harold Liver as an officer cadet in 1915 learning to fly the Avro

now just what the Blackburn factories in Leeds and then Brough could do to win wars."

It is almost impossible for us to imagine how vulnerable these pilots were in the First World War and how flimsy their aircraft were. After all the Wright brothers' first flight in 1903 was only in the air for a few yards, and by 1914 just keeping the machine in the air was something of a miracle – never mind having to fire a gun at the same time.

Youngsters including myself in the 1940s enjoyed reading about Biggles the First World War fighter ace written by Captain W E Johns who himself saw action above the trenches. W E Johns survived the war but the majority of these young pilots did not. Nellie Carbis gave me a photograph of Harold Liver in his uniform as an officer cadet learning to fly in 1915. He was killed in 1917.

This was also the tale of another young pilot who wrote a diary of his battle in the sky and which has been preserved thanks to Kathleen Dabb of Scarborough. Alas there was no name in the diary but there are graphic descriptions of the dogfights. This account has even more relevance than the Biggles novels. What a pity we do not know who he was.

The development of the early days of aviation in Yorkshire was due to the ambitions and abilities of one man: Robert Blackburn. His family were based in Leeds and made their fortune in the production of steam-driven heavy vehicles, especially road rollers.

In 1908 the young Robert had become fascinated by flying and wanted not only to copy but to improve upon the exploits of Bleriot, the Frenchman who was the first man to fly over the English Channel in 1908. The beaches along the Yorkshire coast, especially in the Filey area, proved ideal testing grounds. The first Blackburn aircraft took to the air as early as 1909. His designs were so good that his production sites, first at Leeds and later at Brough near Hull, were never short of orders. Brough is still in production to this day.

Orders were pouring in by the start of the

right a Blackburn Tri-Plane in 1915

below Robert Blackburn standing (far right) in front of the Blackburn Mercury I monoplane in a hanger at Filey

First World War, and monoplanes, biplanes and even triplanes were coming off the assembly lines. At first the authorities preferred the biplane formats which were slower but were much easier to manoeuvre in a 'dog fight'.

The Blackburn Company also built seaplanes which did good service as U-boat spotters. They could cover more ground than the slow-moving airships, although the latter did have a much longer range. The seaplanes, however, could spot U-boats but could not bomb or depth charge them.

The Blackburn Company responded by building the Kangaroo which was not, however, perfected until 1919. It did show the way forward in the development of the torpedo bomber. The Kangaroo was a biplane which was fitted with two Rolls Royce Falcon II engines which were air-cooled, had twelve cylinders and could generate 250-horse power. This proved beyond doubt that there was a future in the production of anti-submarine bombers. It was machines like the Kangaroo which kept the Blackburn Company in profit when many of its rivals went into liquidation.

right & below The Blackburn Kangaroo, 1919

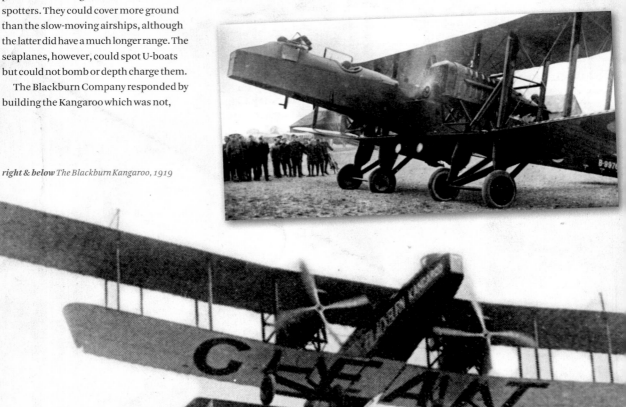

The horrors of the Front

Every time I pass a war memorial, I spare more than a thought for those who died in the blood-and-mud battles of the trenches. Neither should we forget the background organisations and training which went on to prepare young men to face the 'Front'.

Glenda Chapples, who was ninety-three when I interviewed her in 1987, told me:

"My Uncle Tom worked on the Rochdale Canal and was based around Sowerby Bridge. He could turn his hand to owt to do with watter and 'osses. When war started in 1914 he volunteered to fight and was put into the engineers. By 1915 he were training young lads to build and repair bridges, and to get young 'osses used to travelling in boats crossing rivers. He went to a training camp near Lake Windermere. He remembered that they had just launched a new ferry boat and years later he gave a photograph of this to my brother. He took Uncle Fred to see the ferry in 1952 which was still working at that time. He died the following year."

This ferry was replaced in 1954 and had been steam operated; Fred Chapples' expertise with 'engines and osses' must have been a real asset.

It was not just the fighting troops who 'did their bit', as Joe Arter recalls:

"My father John Arter was a butler at Badsworth Grange and was also in a rifle club. At the outbreak of First World War he volunteered and was enlisted at Pontefract Barracks; having some knowledge of a rifle he was made a sergeant straight away. He was sent to the trenches where he was badly wounded at Passchendaele.

He was sent home and, being unfit to return, he was sent to Gisburn in North Yorkshire where he worked on the land helping the farmers."

Those who did not go through the horrors of the trenches can never imagine the tension, and it is both amazing and humbling to record that some were able

above *Volunteer soldiers at Pontefract Barracks*

to have some appreciation of beauty around the battlefields. Captain Raymond Hepper wrote on 2nd February 1916 that, in spite of bursting Very lights,

> "there is an owl which screams like the appeal of a lost soul"

and on March 13th he wrote:

> "The day is perfect, the birds are singing everywhere and if one did not hear the occasional burst of a Hun shell or our own artillery reply ... he could dream that he was at home."

Whilst some sought solace in the everlasting appeal of the natural world, even more reacted by fighting with humour. I have a German friend who once said to me:

> "I know why you won two wars. It was not just because of your armed forces – it was because of your sense of humour."

When I visit him at home I have to sit through hours of *Dads' Army* tapes, and all of his family join in.

He may well have been right if you look at the thousands of postcards which were produced at that time. They are a wonderful mix of sentimentality and humour.

left Captain Raymond Hepper (left) with colleagues at the end of training in Ilkley, December 1915

...t sorrow, heart, sweetheart
...t a soldier's love bear soldier's part.
...think how glad the day will be
...en thy soldier lad comes back to thee.

There is ever and ever so much t...
When I write to my soldier far a...
Perhaps I shall tell it all some...

I wonder if there is anyone else in the...
doing anything besides me!

The dangers of gas

One of the most deadly killers of the First World War was the chlorine-based gas. Both sides used it in the trenches and the effect was often devastating. My wife's grand-father, Sergeant Ben Birchenough, wrote to his wife in 1916 (just before he was killed), which puts the whole of this horrendous period into some sort of context:

"*I am keeping in the best of health and feeling fine and fit for anything. I scarcely know what to write as I have to be so careful. If we put anything down which is not allowed,* *the letter is in danger of being torn up by the censor.*

"*Since I came out here I have been through a class of instruction in the use of the gas helmet for the defence against gas attack. We were put through the whole business, even so far as being closed up in a dugout and having the full force of the gas turned on. It was surprising the effect the gas had on our clothing, especially the buttons which turned green and black, but the helmets were splendid. So you can see*

Sergeant Ben Birchenough and family; he wrote vividly of life at the Front

that we are keeping busy out here, as I have to lecture to 'the boys' on the same subject. We had our initiation into the real stuff last night."

All this shows how brave these lads were. The trauma faced by families in this war was more devastating than in all others before or since. This was because men volunteered en mass and were formed into locally based units. These became known as the 'Pals Regiments' and they went into battle together. The young men of whole villages, mills, factories and churches volunteered, served at the Front and were killed together.

It was reading Ben Birchenough's letter and looking at the woollen mill scenery around Bradford that prompted my wife and I to visit the battlefields of First World War. They are right to say that one picture is worth a thousand words as we looked at re-enactments in the trenches, visited the war graves and looked at pictures of brave men at the Front.

Let us never ever forget those whose pieces were never fully woven.

Caring for the wounded

There is always a tendency, as there always should be, to record those who died in battle. We should never forget, however, those who were wounded. Olive Harwood recalled:

"I worked as a nurse when the troop trains were coming in full of injured young lads. They were transported to hospitals, and I remember the huge wards and all the patients seemed to be smoking."

There were makeshift hospitals all over Yorkshire. Most have never been fully documented, but thankfully a few have.

Ian Dewhirst of Keighley records his local war hospital, which treated 13,214 patients between 1916 and 1919. The hospital was located at Morton Banks close to the River Aire. Private Sharp was a patient in J Ward which was a temporary structure containing 158 beds. One of those looking after the

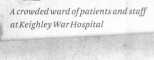

A crowded ward of patients and staff at Keighley War Hospital

84 THE KING AT THE FRONT. The King meets a hospital matron

Grand Duchess George (right) at an entertainment for wounded soldiers in 1916

Grand Duchess George unveils a war memorial to the servicemen who died of their injuries while in her Harrogate hospitals

Grand Duchess George's first hospital for military wounded was on the Tewit Park Estate in Harrogate; she is in the centre of the photograph

Wounded troops had to readjust to life back at home

injured was Miss Annie Collett who kept an autograph book. This was signed by many soldiers of the Prince of Wales's Own Yorkshire regiment, and their sense of humour shines through like a beacon.

Some hospitals were set up and funded by wealthy people. This was certainly the case in Harrogate. Her Imperial Highness Marie Georgievna the Grand Duchess George (1876–1940), who was the daughter of King George I of Greece and related to our own royal family, set up at least four military hospitals in the town.

The Keighley and Harrogate hospitals highlight the need for more and more diligent researchers to delve deeply into the archives and produce a more comprehensive list of First World War hospitals, not just in Yorkshire but all over Britain.

A gift to the armed forces

'We will be home for Christmas' was a widely held belief at the onset of the war in 1914. This was very much misplaced. As that first wartime Christmas approached, the whole nation rose in support of its servicemen and women, and funded a gift consisting of an embossed brass box containing a pipe, lighter, an ounce of tobacco and twenty cigarettes in distinctive monographed wrappers. Non-smokers and boys received a bullet-shaped pencil and a packet of sweets. Nurses were given chocolate.

An advertisement first appeared in the national press in November inviting the public to contribute to a Sailors' and Soldiers' Christmas Fund which had been created by Princess Mary, the seventeen-year-old daughter of George V and who later became the Countess of Harewood. The response was overwhelming.

Princess Mary visiting a military hospital in 1923, a time when the RAF Nursing Service was being renamed in her honour

Many of the items were despatched separately because, once the standard issue of pipe, tobacco and cigarettes was placed in the tin, there was no room for anything else. The tin, pictured right, was five inches (13cm) long and three and a half inches (9cm) wide. It had the princess's profile and an M monogram on the lid above the words 'Christmas 1914.' Around the edge the allies of the time were listed: Belgium, Japan, Montenegro and Serbia, France and Russia. All the boxes also contained a Christmas card and a picture of the princess.

Those which were not distributed until after Christmas were sent out with a card wishing the recipient a victorious New Year. Those wounded and in hospital or on leave, as well as widows and parents who had

lost loved ones, were also entitled to the gift. Prisoners of war had theirs reserved until they were repatriated.

An already stretched postal service made great efforts to distribute the gifts and more than 355,000 were delivered on time, but a shortage of brass meant that many did not receive their gift until 1916; this was obviously because so much brass

was demanded in the production of shells. An inferior alloy had to be substituted, and orders for brass strips were sent to America (a large consignment was lost when the *Lusitania* was sunk).

When the fund finally closed in 1920 almost £200,000 had been donated and more than 2.5 million boxes had been delivered.

Soldiers and nurses with a sign expressing a heartfelt belief

THE DAY WAR BROKE OUT

Peace in our time?

One of my first memories of a lifetime of collecting photographs was in 1946 on my tenth birthday. This was an image of a German Zeppelin seen flying over my home town of Barrow-in-Furness and taken in 1936. This flight was described as a courtesy visit. My godmother, Doris Dickinson, who was a postmistress, said:

"From 1935 onwards the so-called 'German Tourists' flooded into Britain, and their demands were such that the shops soon ran out of maps and guidebooks. One other thing which seemed strange to me was that, unlike normal tourists, they did not send postcards but sealed letters, often with photographs inside them. At this time my father was one of the port missionaries in Hull, and he told me that the Hindenburg had been flying all over Yorkshire and that German tourists were visiting the docks."

These flights over Yorkshire were seen by many people, including Eric Shippin:

"I believe that the Hindenburg did pass over Leeds on more than one occasion. I was living in Holbeck at the time. Colour film had recently become available and Clarkson's chemist, then located at the junction between Cemetery Road and Elland Road in Holbeck, displayed a few colour photos in their shop … The country was gearing up for war with Germany and rumour had it that the airship had chosen to fly over the area on a spy mission."

The Hindenburg photographed in 1936 en route to Yorkshire

The Hindenburg over Farsley, Leeds

There was no doubt about this. Alec Taylor recalls:

"I attended Leeds Technical School off Cookridge Street. At lunchtime I came home by bus along Burley Road and as we were turning into Cardigan Road, there it was: the Hindenburg, hovering low between Armley Road and Kirkstall Road. There were factories on Armley Road, a railway junction going west and the other north over a large viaduct by the side of a gasometer. By the side of the junction was the canal which, if breached, would flood the river Aire below. Kirkstall Road also had factories including the British Screw works … During the war bombs were dropped between Kirkstall Road and Burley Road."

All this proves beyond any doubt is that the Hindenburg was a spy in the sky; German photographs discovered after the war showed this quite clearly. There were many sightings of the Hindenburg all over Yorkshire.

M. Robertson of Hull was born in *"the village of Cawood not far from York and was walking by the River Ouse … I suddenly heard an eerie noise. Glancing up and not very high was this shape; never having seen an airship you can imagine how I felt. At this time it was rumoured that it was spying on Church Fenton aerodrome which is not far away."*

Ernest Astley of York remembers the Hindenburg flying over Keighley and it *"dropped a package over the centre of Keighley which contained a wreath to be placed on the graves of German soldiers who were buried at Morton cemetery in the town during the First World War".*

This proved that the crew of the Hindenburg were highly trained and that their navigation was spot-on. It was sightings such as these, as well as the very obvious build-up of tension all over Europe, which indicated to most people in power that Neville Chamberlain was both naïve and wrong. There would not be "Peace in our time" but we would all soon be saying "The day war broke out".

The Hindenburg passes over South Craven in May 1936

The Hindenburg (D-LZ129), with the Olympics rings of the 1936 Games visible on the side

At war with Germany

Although I was only three at the time, I have a very vague memory of Sunday 3rd September 1939. My family were gathered round the radio. At 11.15am the Prime Minister Neville Chamberlain broadcast to the nation those fateful words: "This country is at war with Germany". My mother went into the kitchen to prepare lunch but she had left a gas tap partly turned on. When she lit the cooker there was a huge bang and a flash, which thankfully only singed her eyebrows! It was this bang which I can still remember and I am said to have shouted "Has Hitler come?"

Dennis Goode of Knaresborough also remembers that day:

"I was a boy messenger – a Penny Runner – for the GPO. During the preceding few months I'd delivered many unwelcome telegrams calling up the unemployed to dig air-raid shelters and of course members of the Army Territorials, naval and air force reservists etc.

"On 3rd September 1939 everyone had their ears 'glued' to the wireless, though the announcement that we were at war with Germany came as no surprise ... there was a little fear ... Just to alarm everybody the sirens sounded soon after the news broadcast.

"Less than fifty minutes later there was a postman knocking on our door with a telegram ordering me to report for work as soon as possible – and to bring a meal and my gas mask. I remember cycling down from Woodbank Place, Manningham, to Bradford Head Post Office as fast as I was able ... I don't remember how long I stayed on duty, but I do remember that when I did arrive home my mother and father had fixed in place the blackout blinds which they had prepared the previous week."

Folk like Dennis Goode lost loved ones but kept going, but the words of the song *Keep Smiling Through* kept the spirits alive. Comedians like Rob Wilton ensured that people did not just smile but actually laughed. As soon as the music hall audiences heard him say "The day war broke out ..." the whole place roared the next line "... my missus said to me".

'If invasion comes, we will fight'

Many people in Britain knew that the German spies were good at their job. As well as the Hindenburg flights, there were German tourists enjoying the sights – or should it be sites – of Britain.

The Hitler Youth organised cycling tours but they seemed to concentrate their attentions on factories rather than beauty spots. A favourite was Sheffield and its steelworks, including the only

factory which could produce the metal of the quality needed for use in a small part of the Rolls Royce Merlin engine.

Invasion committees were set up in each area, and each had its own designated war

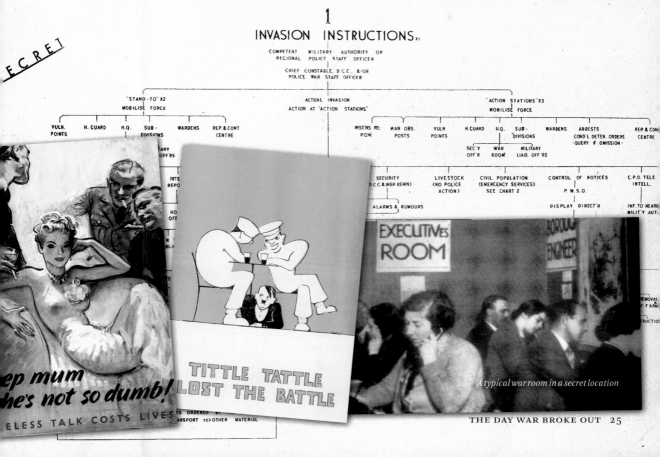

A typical war room in a secret location

room containing operational plans which were kept under lock and key.

Apart from the invasion committees, detailed plans were prepared involving men with a knowledge of explosives such as miners and quarrymen. I became friends with Colonel Wright who specialised in logistics and ballistics before his retirement from the army. At his home in Grassington he told me:

"The German invaders would have found it difficult, if not impossible, to deal with these small groups of ex-miners. Providing they were kept supplied with food and ammunition, they could have carried out strategic attacks and literally disappeared underground."

The authorities were also well aware of the importance of communications. All sorts of plans were put in hand, and men used to racing motorcycles were put on red alert. Men such as John Warburton and Albert Gillings were soon contacted. John had garages in Blackpool and Leeds, and he rode in the Isle of Man TT races, with Albert as his mechanic. Both were keen on the sport of motorcycle scrambling across rugged country tracks. They were recruited in secret and were on standby in the event of invasion.

One other group which was placed on high alert were the racing pigeon fanciers. The best birds were supplied with 'rations of grain' and would have been taken to release points close to potential invasion sites. When this event was observed, the pigeons were released and, once arrived at the roosts, the messages would be passed on to a central control office and plans adapted accordingly.

Men such as Albert Gillings and John Warburton were recruited in secret to combat the threatened invasion

Pigeons were a valuable war weapon

Guarding the coast

The lighthouses at Spurn proved to be essential; observation posts were established on these and troops were based in huts. Gerald Woods was in the RAF in 1939, and his brother was an electrician working at Spurn and in secret. He told me:

"I was on leave and I went with my brother to Spurn Head, a haunt of ours as kids when we went fishing and catching rabbits ... I found lots of anti-invasion preparations. A new road was being built, there were pillboxes everywhere and huge concrete blocks placed in positions to prevent the movement of heavy vehicles. A team of Royal Engineers were in residence, who were trained not only to build but also able to destroy installations if the Germans gained any sort of foothold."

The Humber estuary between the ports of Grimsby and Hull was vulnerable, and the problem areas were addressed by constructing a system of fortifications set into the seabed and looking very like modern-day oil platforms. The forts were at Haile and Bull Sands, and they were manned by Royal Artillery Coastal Regiments. These would have been a deterrent to U-boats engaged in mining the approaches to the docks.

right *Fortifications were constructed all along the Yorkshire coast*

far right *The Spurn lighthouses were ideal observation posts*

below right *The offshore forts were manned by the Royal Artillery Coastal Regiments*

Offshore forts were built at haile and Bull Sands in the Humber Estuary

Evacuees

At the start of the war, with the memories of the battles and slaughter in the trenches of only twenty years before, everyone was certain that the Germans would drop canisters of poison gas as well as bombs on our towns and cities. Those whose job it was to plan our defences thought that very many children would perish. This accounts for the mass evacuation of children from urban to rural areas.

Each child had to pack clothes, and carry their gas mask case on a string and also an identity label. Once the frightened kids had arrived at their destination they had to be 'processed', which meant finding local families to take in these extra guests.

Eric Jones of South Elmsall near Leeds remembers this time very well:

"I was eight when war was declared on 3rd September 1939 and can remember listening to the wireless with my parents on that Sunday knowing that something was happening, but not quite understanding just what it was.

"However, my war had begun three days earlier on the Friday night. My friend Jim (now dead) and I had been playing on the newly constructed air-raid shelter behind Broad Lane School ... At the top of our estate we came across a crowd of people with a number of strange children. I say strange because, being a small mining village, everyone knew everyone else but these children were strange to us. It became obvious that these children were going away with people we knew which, even to our young minds, seemed odd. We dashed home ... and I shouted to my dad that 'They are giving kids away in our street'. This must have intrigued him, and he put on his hat and coat to see what was happening; he came back later with a brother and sister – Ronnie and Margaret Sidebottom from Leeds."

Evacuated children board a train to safety

TAKE THEM BACK!
TAKE THEM BACK!...
TAKE THEM BACK!...

DON'T do it
Moth

LEAVE THE CHIL
WHERE THEY A

ISSUED BY THE MINISTRY O

Eric Jones's memories of evacuees involved happy memories, but this was not always the case and for some of these disrupted children it really was a case of taking pot luck.

A great deal of organisation was needed in order to place these children in safe billets and the village women, usually members of the WI or the local vicars' wives, played a vital role. Some of these ladies had led very sheltered lives. One vicar's wife made notes on each evacuee as they arrived to be sorted. Against some she wrote 'VD' and it was only later that someone realised that this was the lady's very own shorthand for 'Very Dirty'.

I remember evacuees arriving at my local village. We very soon realised that these kids were much tougher than us and we learned not to pick fights with the 'townies' – and this was only the girls!

Some evacuees really did fall on their feet but few could rival the billet allotted to Marie Caltieri of Keighley:

"I was three days off my eleventh birthday when war was declared. My father (who had been gassed in the First World War)

The first evacuees arrive in Scarborough on 1st September 1939

Evacuees head off in numbers to safety

and my mother thought it would be wise to have me evacuated to a place of relative safety … *several Leeds children were evacuated to the more rural areas of Yorkshire, but we had no idea where we would end up. It was quite a traumatic time for me as it would be the first time I had been away from my parents … The coach arrived and we waved our parents goodbye*

"*Our destination was Boston Spa, just an hour or so from Leeds. Once there we were herded into the village hall, given a carrier bag containing rations and told to sit down until we were 'given' to families … I was taken with a 'new girl' who came from Harrogate to our temporary home, Lane End, a large detached house in its own extensive grounds.*

"*To a city child from a working-class area of Leeds, it was a revelation: our own playroom, staff quarters for the cook and maids, a daily gardener and chauffeur, a Rolls Royce and a second car, not to mention two kerry blue dogs, greenhouses, a swing, a see-saw and a paddling pool … Suddenly I found myself transported into a world of which I knew nothing.*"

On the whole the rural folk treated the children well, but they did have the threat of not one invasion but two. The German onslaught did not materialise but the evacuee invasion certainly did.

Hull evacuees having fun in the Yorkshire countryside

OFFICIAL INSTRUCTIONS ISSUED BY THE MINISTRY OF HOME SECU

GAS ATTACK

HOW TO PUT ON YOUR GAS MASK

Always keep your ~~s~~ mask with you ~~d~~ay and night. ~~L~~arn to put it on ~~qu~~ickly. ~~Pra~~ctise wearing it.

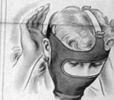

1. Hold your breath.   2. Hold mask in front of face, with thumbs inside straps.
3. Thrust chin well forward into mask, pull straps over head as far as they will go.
4. Run finger round facepiece taking care head-straps are not twisted.

THE GAS RATTLES SOUND

The Home Guard

Crucial to the repelling of any invasion force was the efficiency of what eventually became the Home Guard. Winston Churchill was not only a wordsmith but he was very much a man of action. Anthony Eden was appointed the Minister for War and he announced the formation of the Local Defence Volunteers. The LDV was soon known as 'Look, Duck and Vanish'. By the end of May 250,000 men had volunteered; by July that number had doubled and the Volunteers had been renamed the Home Guard.

At first there were too few tools available. Geoff Cain remembers that

"museums holding First World War weapons handed them over to old men who had either made them, fixed them or actually fired them. Soon they were

Guarding the mills was vital war work

"Let 'em all come"

MEN
41-55

HOME DEFENCE
BATTALIONS

H. G.

HOME GUARD
MANUAL
1941

polished and working. We were given an old Vickers machine gun and some ammo. I had worked at Vickers and I knew about this model and just how lethal it could be."

Soon a limited supply of 'proper' weapons and ammunition began to arrive, and there was a significant hardcore of very able young soldiers who would have made life very tough for German paratroopers, who would themselves only be very lightly armed and briefed to capture and hold a strategic point until the main invading force arrived. Harry Collins recalls:

"I were a lad at the time living near the railway at Doncaster. The works had its own Home Guard units, and there were squads working on or near all railway stations and goods yards. Who better to protect the rail network than the chaps who had spent their lives manning them?"

A few Home Guard Units were given what can now be referred to as SAS-style training. Units of about six men were made ready to literally disappear into the bowels of the earth, equipped with the latest radio sets and with sealed orders which were only to be opened when the password 'Cromwell' indicated that the invasion had begun. There were also lists of a very few individuals who had Nazi sympathies. These are kept very secret even to this day but Eric Halsall recalls that "we had a bumping-off list".

By the time Dunkirk was over, men were waiting to hear the password 'Cromwell' which meant that the invasion forces had landed and that the Home Guard had to resist the intruders. We should all enjoy the Dads' Army fun and games but it must never be forgotten that there was a deeply secret side to these events. There would not have been many German soldiers who would have stood up to an angry Yorkshire miner with a Sten gun and a belt full of hand grenades.

Training in unarmed combat

Training with a Vickers machine gun

'EBOMB
TZ'

BRITAIN
SHALL NOT
BURN

TAIN'S FIRE GUARD IS B

GAS
DEFLATION

THE BLITZ

A·R·P

'The bomber will always get through'

As early as 1936, Prime Minister Stanley Baldwin commented that 'the bomber will always get through'. Whilst this did prove to be the case, bomber crews had few electronic aids and relied upon visual clues. Those on the ground knew that showing a light could prove fatal.

This was the reason for imposing the 'blackout'. This operated from the minute war was declared and continued in operation until 17th September 1944. Blackout was total and initially there were many accidents, some of them fatal. In an attempt to reduce accidents, shop corners, kerbs, steps and vehicle running boards and bumpers were painted white, and so were the bases of some tree trunks. I can remember being told to stop for a few minutes when I went out in the dark to let my eyes become accustomed to the dark conditions.

Efforts were made to adjust the working hours of daylight by introducing first single and then double summer time, so that the working day utilised more hours of daylight; this also reduced the number of accidents. These adjustments were noticed by those who worked in the open air, such as Laura Parkinson who was a Land Army girl:

> "For us it was always a dawn to dusk job, and the shifting of the clocks also meant that we could enjoy what little bit of leisure time which was available to us."

The Yorkshire Blitz

	dates of main raids	number of bombers	death toll
HULL	18th March 1941	75	
	7th, 8th May 1941	100	
	17th July 1941	75	1,055
SHEFFIELD	12th December 1940	100+	
	15th December 1940	75+	624
LEEDS	14th March 1941		65

There were other Yorkshire targets and some on the coast

	number of raids	civilians killed	buildings damaged
BRIDLINGTON	30	24	3,000
SCARBOROUGH	17	30	2,250

Gracious Lord, oh bomb the Germans
Spare the women for thy sake
And if this is not too easy
We will pardon thy mistake
But Gracious Lord, what e'er shall be
Don't let anyone bomb me.

JOHN BETJEMAN

Bombs over Yorkshire

The main thrust of the Luftwaffe attacks on Yorkshire were focussed upon Sheffield and Hull, but most parts of the county had occasional attacks which in their own way were every bit as traumatic.

J Morrell has clear memories of the bombs which fell on Doncaster:

"At the time we thought that they were aiming at the colliery and if so they were not far off their target because one landed in a lime pit only 150 yards away. They may also have been aiming at the locomotive works. A later raid dropped a parachute mine which fell on houses in Royston avenue at Bentley. Fourteen people were killed and there is a memorial to them in the nearby cemetery at Arksey."

Eileen Sykes of Leeds recalls

"Just before the war Kirkstall Forge was converted into an armaments factory and I worked there. I was there during the bombing of the factory in August 1942. I remember watching the flares coming down ... then came the bombs ...

I got hit in the hand with a piece of shrapnel but luckily I was not badly injured. Six people were killed in this bombing. It was a terrible night."

The coastal towns also saw action. Bridlington was a target and one which does need to be explained. Some think that the white cliffs of Flamborough Head were used by the German bombers as a landmark. If for whatever reason they failed to find their target and had to keep an eye on their fuel levels, they dropped their bombs on the closest town to Flamborough Head, which was Bridlington. I have looked carefully at German documents and Bridlington was never listed as a specific target. The main bombing, however, took place on the 10th and 11th July 1940; 24 civilians were killed and 3,000 houses were damaged. The area around Hilderthorpe Road was devastated and the Cozy Corner Hotel was found not to be so cosy! The reaction of the people of Bridlington, as elsewhere in Britain, was predictable. They put their hands in their pockets and provided funds for a fleet of Austin K2 ambulances which were constructed for the army.

All through the Blitz, Yorkshire folk could be relied on to 'do their bit'.

above Smouldering ruins of Goddard, Walker and Brown's in Queen Street where several lives were lost

right Shattered masonry of Hull's GPO falls across Alfred Gelder Street

The Hull Blitz

Phil Penfold makes a point which has seldom been focused upon:

"It was on 7th September 1940 that 340 German bombers reached their target for the night – London ... when they finally left for home they left 436 dead and 1,666 injured, damaged port and dock facilities, and fires raging in the East End ... but it is a mistake to believe that this was the very first raid in the UK. Birmingham, Edinburgh, Liverpool and Hull had been targeted in late August ... the citizens of Hull were getting used to air-raid warnings.

"The first raid had been in June 1940 and by the night of 27th August, they'd had their sixtieth."

No city outside London had faced such a pounding and, apart from the 1,055 people who lost their lives, 86,715 of the 92,000 houses in the city were totally destroyed or

above *Rescue work in Hull, May 1941*

left *Costello's Corner at the junction of Jameson and Sackville Street*

Esther Baker worked at the Central Fire Station in Hull:

"The incoming calls told us of familiar streets, burning furiously, of buildings we'd known since childhood reduced to rubble. We knew that out there ... wardens and rescue squads were battling to dig out survivors and our own fire-fighters were struggling to contain a hundred conflagrations with insufficient water because the river was low or the mains were smashed."

There can be very few schoolboys who kept diaries during the Blitz, but one very valuable exception was Derry Jones:

"Air raids were heaviest in 1940 but from 1940 to 1945, the city, easily identifiable from the air, received over eighty attacks with bombs, incendiaries, parachute mines and even cannon fire from the Luftwaffe pilots.

"After a raid early on 24th June 1943, I walked into town from school at lunch-time with my friend Bob Fewlass and we found fires still burning at the City Museum, at a brewery and Costello's store which contained furniture saved from what was left of Blaydons store.

"On the night of 2nd-3rd March 1945 the windows of our house in Brickwell Avenue and its neighbours were shot up by aircraft cannon shells."

damaged, and more than 150,000 were forced to find temporary accommodation.

One aspect of Hull's Civil Defence work which has a place in history is what has become known as the Hull Lift Method. Men involved in the building trade developed techniques for releasing people from collapsed buildings. They worked out how they could lift off a roof using an adapted crane before the building collapsed and trapped people underneath. The Ministry of Home Security called this the Hull Lift Method, and it was adapted for use all over the country.

Sheffield in the Blitz

It is easy to believe even when we look at the statistics on the Blitz that the authorities expected the 'butcher's bill' to be much higher than actually proved to be the case. Cardboard coffins, makeshift mortuaries and mass grave sites were organised but in the end were not required. It also has to be remembered at this point in time there was no National Health Service, but many cities including Sheffield reacted in a very positive manner and organised a surprisingly efficient ambulance service. All these plans proved to have been well worth the effort, when in December 1940 bombs rained down on the city.

Phil Penfold comments that *"Sheffield's turn came just as the city was preparing for Christmas. Then, the city had a population of around 560,000 and was a vital cog in the British war machine, as a centre of steel production. There were also many major armament makers all contributing to the war effort ... Later at the end of the war, top-secret German documents were captured and it was plain that the main targets were places like the Atlas Steel Works, the Brown Bayley works, the River Don and Meadowhall Works, the Tinsley Park collieries and the Orgreave Coke works ...*

on the nights of 12th and 15th December Sheffield was going to be an ideal target and [the Germans] called the plan for the raids 'Operation Crucible'."

Doris Billington, who lived at Whiston, remembers the Sheffield Blitz. She was eighteen at the time and worked at Day's bakery in Castle Street, Sheffield:

"I set off at 6am and boarded a tram to Sheffield. I had heard the heavy bombing the night before and when I got into Sheffield the place was a shambles. There were fires everywhere and we were told that some tram and bus crews had been killed but there were still bodies lying in the streets, some of them badly burned.

"On the Sunday the sirens went again and incendiary bombs set fire to the church roof and a haystack. One fell in our gar-

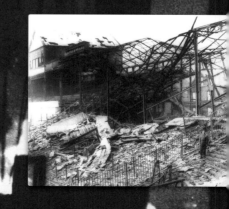

above Sheffield after German bombing

right Damage to Scott Road and Grimesthorpe Road, Sheffield

above A body removed from a blitzed building

den but we put it out by throwing earth from the top of our Anderson shelter on top of the flaming nuisance.

"I'll never forget what the Germans did to our beautiful city."

Charles Green of Rawmarsh near Rotherham also remembers the Sheffield Blitz: "I was a teenager at the time of the bombing and actually thrilled by the sound. But when I found out what happened to Sheffield its steelworks, the damage and the loss of life, I grew into a man overnight. I hoped that we would soon get our own back!"

A young Roy Hattersley remembers being led out into his back garden to be shown the crimson night sky. "It was a terrible, awesome and frightening sight."

This captures in one sentence just what the folk of Sheffield had to put up with, and then just get on with their lives. I will never cease to be amazed at the sheer resilience of everyday people during the Blitz.

opposite Bramall Lane 'blitzed'

left Bomb damage in Sheffield, December 1940

Air-raid shelters

My own very first recollections of the bombing were of sitting in an Anderson shelter and listening to bombs falling and ack-ack guns replying. These shelters and all the others gave a real sense of security.

The Anderson shelter was by far the most common refuge, and it was a perfect example of structure related to function. The Home Secretary at that time was Sir John Anderson and on 10th November 1938 he commissioned an engineer named William Paterson, who had a very able assistant called David Anderson, to design a cheap yet functional shelter as soon as possible. The design was delivered within one week, and in total around 2,300,000 Anderson shelters were produced. People who earned less than £250 were given their shelter free but the more affluent had to pay £7. The shelter consisted of fourteen sheets of corrugated iron which had to be bolted together.

Dennis Woodrow remembers his Anderson shelter:

"Folk were told to cover their shelter with the earth which had been dug out of the hole. To say the least they were damp and sometimes flooded. My dad was a joiner and he lined the floor with sawdust. Some people like us did make them quite comfortable and for years after the war ours was the perfect garden shed. We continued to grow vegetables and flowers in the soil which covered the roof."
Anderson shelters could only be

far left *Christmas in an Anderson shelter*

middle left *'God bless our Anderson shelter', Leeds 1940*

supplied to those people who had gardens, and so the Morrison shelter was designed to be erected inside the house. This had a solid steel top mounted on solid legs and the structure could therefore function as a dining room table. By the end of 1941 some 500,000 Morrison shelters were in use. Edith Collins remembers her home in Sheffield when

> *"my sister Margaret and me had cosy beds under the shelter and even if there was no raid on we still wanted to sleep in our den. Long after the war we still used our 'table' and the cat always slept under it."*

In areas which were densely populated neither the Anderson or the Morrison shelters were appropriate, and so brick shelters were constructed. Bob Kirkwood who was a policeman in Hull at the time remembers:

> *"There is no doubt that these communal shelters were a boost to morale when a raid was imminent … We also knew that at times these shelters were a nightmare. Gangs of crooks could collect in them, courting couples did what courting couples do, and even worse the shelters were used as public conveniences."*

Most large factories and shops constructed communal shelters, situated mostly in their basements. Seats were provided and facilities to brew up were sometimes literally 'on tap'.

Consol shelters accommodated one or two people and resembled huge shells or reinforced sentry boxes – which is just what they were. They were designed for use by those who were on duty when the Blitz was at its height. They were used around docks, railway junctions, armament factories and other particularly vulnerable areas. Geoff Copeland recalls

> *"One night when I was on fire duty at Hull docks I did feel very safe even when the bombs began to fall. I do remember once when three of us – two ARP lads and me – crushed into one shelter and told rude jokes as the bombs crashed down. When we came out fires were blazing every-where and our metal shelter was so hot that we could hardly bear to touch it."*

above left *A newly constructed Anderson shelter in Baildon*

above *A municipal street shelter surviving bomb damage, 15th March 1941, Model Road, Armley, Leeds*

The threat of gas attacks

Nobody knew in Britain whether gas would be used or not. Everyone was provided with a gas mask and the demand for rubber was almost insatiable during the early years of the war. There was still the usual British sense of humour at work, and enterprising businesses made masks for pets such as dogs, cats and horses.

There was, however, a very serious side to the gas threat as John Chippendale well remembers:

"I was almost six when war was declared … and as I lived at Boroughbridge, just three miles south of the Dishforth aerodrome, we had to take air-raid warnings very seriously. We all carried gas masks to school in cardboard containers but they rapidly disintegrated and were replaced by canvas ones. Babies were provided with 'live-in' masks and air was pumped into them via a filter and using little hand-bellows."

In order to detect even the slightest presence of gas, a very primitive warning system was devised. Wooden boards were placed in some streets and treated with a special paint. If these boards changed colour from green to orange, then there was gas in the air.

In the event there was nothing but 'normal' bombs in the air, but if you ask people to recall their memories of the war the first object they mention is invariably the gas mask.

above *Chris Chippendale pumping air to nine-month-old brother Michael in a baby gas mask*

left *The ARP prepare*

above Sheffield ARP wardens

Beat 'FIREBOMB FRITZ'

BRITAIN SHALL NOT BURN

...AIN'S FIRE GUARD IS BRITAIN'S DEFENCE

Civil Defence

These days it is hard to fully realise just how committed people were to give of their time and also risk their lives to help others during the war. Both old and young did their bit to ensure that Britain did not burn and that 'Firebomb Fritz' was finally extinguished.

Many towns had a very well organised Civil Defence messenger corps. There was one very active unit operating in and around Leeds. The unit was initiated as early as 1936 and was organised by the Boy Scouts who proved true to their motto to 'be prepared' to help in the event of an

air-raid. Boys owning their own bicycles were particularly welcomed. The boys were also trained in the rudiments of first aid. The Leeds unit proved to be one of the best, and a film made in the city was used to train boys in other areas all over the country.

We should all enjoy the Dad's Army portrayal of the air-raid warden but these people were not 'Little Hitlers' but often carried out backbreaking and brave work.

Emily Davies remembers the times

when her father-in-law was an ARP warden in Sheffield:

"As he helped out an old lady she seemed to have the largest bosom that he had ever seen and furthermore it wobbled. Once she was on her feet she opened her dressing gown to reveal two small dogs and a cat, all intent on escaping."

The air-raid wardens worked closely with all the other Civil Defence workers, including the bomb disposal squads and the fire services.

Many firemen all over Britain proved to be real heroes, and many lost their lives in the Blitz. At the outbreak of war the service was not organised as a countrywide network but each town and city had its own brigade. They often used equipment which varied in specifications and which were not mutually compatible. John Trelore remembers all too well that

"the equipment was often old and the specifications were such that no two

brigades could work together. In the middle of the Sheffield Blitz some of the water mains fractured but in a few places big inflatable rubber tanks full of water had been set up in readiness. I remember these tanks blistering and some bursting because of the heat. There were also occasions when the water actually boiled and we had to deal with steam as well as the smoke and dust."

left A very rare picture of an unexploded oil bomb

below A brave team of Royal Engineers tackle an unexploded bomb in the centre of Sheffield

below An improvised fire engine blistered in the heat of battle

right An inflatable emergency water tank in use

Barrage balloons

There are conflicting opinions with regard to just how effective barrage balloons were against the German bombers. Was the expense of both time and resources worth it? Dennis Wood is in no doubt and pointed out

"apart from anything else it gave people a sense of security just to see them above their heads".

Barrage balloons were probably one of the most evocative sights associated with

the war. Thousands were produced at factories such as those owned by the Dunlop Company, which were taken over by the Ministry of Supply. Rene Mackintosh of Leeds remembers one of her cousins getting married; her cousin worked in the Dunlop factory and her husband-to-be was working as a supervisor at the balloon testing station at Bowlees, near Halifax.

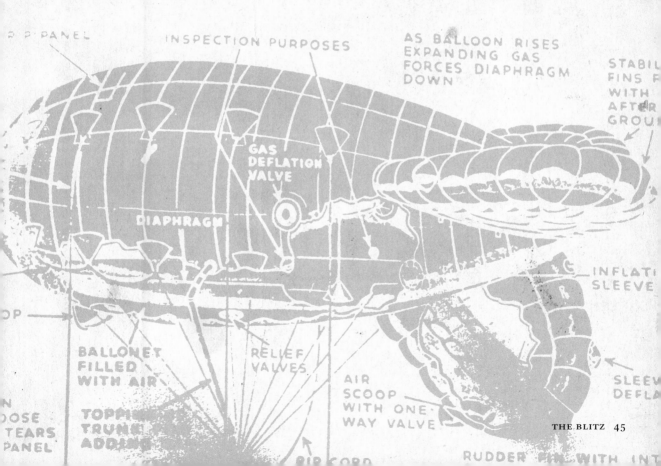

?.P.PANEL

INSPECTION PURPOSES

AS BALLOON RISES EXPANDING GAS FORCES DIAPHRAGM DOWN

STABIL FINS F WITH AFTER GROU

GAS DEFLATION VALVE

DIAPHRAGM

INFLATI SLEEVE

OP

BALLONET FILLED WITH AIR

RELIEF VALVES

AIR SCOOP WITH ONE WAY VALVE

SLEEVE DEFLA

N OOSE TEARS PANEL

TOPPI TRUN ADDIN

RUDDER FI WITH INT

"Even when they were all 'dolled up' for the wedding they both smelled a bit of rubber."

Leading Aircraftsman Horace Birkin, who was based in Hull during 1941 and 1942, remembers:

"I was in charge of a unit near Hull docks. When an air-raid warning sounded our balloons were already up there but we then opened secret orders. These told us to alter the position and especially the height of the balloons. No doubt this meant that the Germans could not predict from previous raids where the balloons were or at what height they were flying ... the balloons did not stop the Blitz doing lots of damage and killing people but it did make them feel safer."

Despite all efforts to prevent it, the occasional balloon did escape and cause chaos. One such escaped over Leeds on 15th May 1940 and provided a very welcome entertainment. Having broken loose from its cables it drifted over the city, knocking chimney pots off houses as it went. Sirens were sounded as if an air-raid was imminent in broad daylight. As the balloon reached St James's Hospital, a group of intrepid RAF men grabbed hold of a cable and secured it to a lamppost. The balloon obviously had a mind of its own: it uprooted the lamppost and was even more of a hazard for the next four hours. Eventually a squad of RAF men finally secured the rampant beast on Sheepscar Road North. A group of boys from the Royal Park School followed the balloon and did not turn up for lessons. On the following morning they were each given 1,000 lines to remind them that "I must not follow barrage balloons".

above LAC Horace Birkin, based in Hull 1940–41

right A barrage balloon being fabricated

"...nday Dispatch" Page To He...
Everyone Defend The Country

THE War Office has issued these diagram pictures of enemy troop-carrying planes. They are intended to guide Local Defence Volunteers and all members of the public.

Some of these pictures have been published elsewhere in the last few days, but this page contains many more details and also silhouettes of comparable British bombers. It is the only complete... Cut it out and hang it on your wall.

If you see an aeroplane that resembles an enemy, tell the ..., an air raid warden or the L.D.V. at once.

Here are some simple points to remember:
If the 'plane has more than two engines it is probably a German.

The 3-engined Junkers Ju 52 has one engine in the nose, looking like the head of a fly. These have been the 'planes most used for parachutists.

The Junkers Ju 90 has wings that sweep backwards like a swallow in flight.

Note the square-cut edges of the wings and tails of the Junkers planes.

If a bomber is flying low in daylight, note the ...
British bombers are mostly painted black on ...
(There are some silver or light green.)

The badge painted on British 'planes is like a r...
blue target, with the red as the bull's-eye.

German bombers are painted light blue-grey ...
tage and wings.

Their badge is a black cross, outlined with a wh...
white band itself is outlined in black.

A black swastika is usually carried on the tail ...

WAR IN THE AIR

...HESE ARE THE TYPES OF GERMAN AIRCRAFT YOU ARE MOST LIKELY TO...

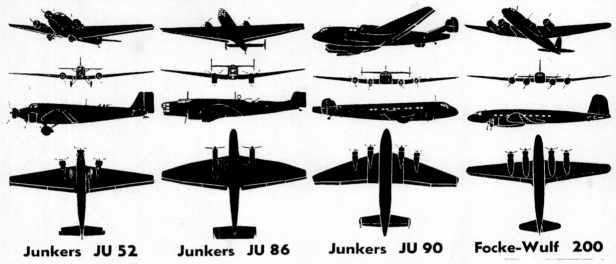

Junkers JU 52   Junkers JU 86   Junkers JU 90   Focke-Wulf 200

Friend or foe?

In these days of peace we tend to think of aircraft in terms of going off on holiday or occasionally seeing and hearing military aircraft on training flights. In the skies all over Britain during the war, it was very different. The aircraft in those days were much slower and there were very many different types: trainers, fighters, bombers, seaplanes, biplanes and monoplanes; and there were both friendly and enemy aircraft.

It is no wonder that members of the Royal Observer Corps (ROC) had to be very skilled. Edwin Barnes of Sheffield recalls:

"My father… became a member of the ROC. He had manuals which he had to study in order to correctly identify the various types of aircraft he saw. His station was high on a hill overlooking the Yorkshire coast and he had a radio with which to contact his base. He also had a direction finder, and developed the skills needed to work out compass bearings, speed and height of the aircraft which he spotted."

It was not only the 'professional' spotters who learned about the various types of aircraft. Newspapers produced identification charts, and aircraft recognition books were printed even before serious hostilities had begun.

The Air Transport Auxiliary

This brave and skilled group of pilots of both sexes ferried all types of aircraft from the factories to operational airfields. They were often called 'shuttle drivers', which is precisely what they were. They had to be able to fly any aircraft without any preliminary training. They had to deliver Wellingtons, Hampdens, Whitleys, Stirlings, Halifaxes and from 1942 onwards the legendary Lancasters. All of the pilots, especially the ladies, loved it when they delivered Spitfires, Hurricanes and Mosquitoes. It was dangerous work, especially as they had no detailed navigational aids and were not in radio contact.

By far the best known of the ATA was Amy Johnson, born at 154 St Georges' Road, Hull, on 1st July 1903. In 1930 her solo flight to Australia in her own Gypsy Moth made her a household name, and she was awarded an MBE by King George V. She was, apparently, not the best of pilots and her bumpy landings became legendary.

It was no surprise that, as war loomed, Amy wanted her flying skills to be put to good use, but it took some time before the authorities realised that women could

A Vickers Wellington

Handley Page Hampden bombers on the assembly line

A Blackburn ROC built at Brough, East Yorkshire

actually be useful as pilots. It may well never have happened had there not been so many young male pilots needed for front-line action.

On 5th January 1941 Amy Johnson became the first of these shuttle pilots to be killed, and her death is still surrounded by a web of controversy. She set off from Blackpool in an Oxford trainer on her way to Kidlington near Oxford. The official view is that she lost her way in bad weather and crashed into the Thames Estuary. There are questions, however, which have never officially been addressed: was she on a secret mission? Was she carrying two extra passengers? And was she shot down by friendly fire?

I once had a conversation with Art Talbot, who knew Amy at the time. He remembers her giving presents to the ground crew which often included Belgian chocolates and French cigarettes. This would seem to support the theory that she was not just operating around the airfields of Britain.

It is not just Amy Johnson who needs to be remembered for her exploits in the ATA. Others who helped us fly to victory include Margaret Fox, Molly Rose, Pauline Gower, Joy Lofthouse, Mary Wilkins Ellers, Wendy Space-Barker and a host of others. The work of the ATA was indeed on 'a wing and a prayer', and many brave men and women were killed.

above Halifax bombers being assembled in 1941

left Amy Johnson with her pilot bag

Blackburn aircraft

The Blackburn Aircraft Company had established its reputation at the start of the First World War, and throughout the whole of the Second World War its aircraft performed invaluable service. Aviation historians will never forget Ripons, Baffins, Sharks, Skuas, ROCS, Bothas and Firebrands plus other types. Hundreds of workers who toiled long hours on the production lines at the Olympia works in Leeds and at Brough on the coast close to Hull have treasured memories of this time.

Edwina Jackson's father worked as an airframe fitter, working mainly on Baffins and Sharks, and he

"always got mad when it was said that all biplanes were obsolete and played no part in the war. The Blackburn biplane bombers and seaplanes inflicted a lot of

left to right Major J D Rennie, G E Petty Major F A Bumpus,

above *The all-secret, all-metal, all-action Blackburn Skua*

right *An operational Shark squadron in the Mediterranean 1943*

below *A Roc in 1943 adapted to serve as a tow for target practice*

damage on German vessels, especially to the U-boats."

The Blackburn design team did produce a monoplane, the all-metal Skua, which was bristling with revolutionary ideas. Whilst it is quite right to celebrate the merits of the Spitfire and the Hurricane, Winston Churchill himself said that

"the Blackburn Skua contributed greatly to Britain's strife towards the defence of its homeland and its ultimate aim of winning the war".

Aircraft assembly at Yeadon

Few of us who nowadays set off on holiday from Leeds Bradford Airport realise that here there was once a huge and very secret aircraft factory. To conceal the works, the flat roofs were covered in soil, planted with grass and fenced off to allow livestock to graze on it.

The site began as RAF Yeadon where 609 Squadron was based from 1936. The AVRO Company developed the site, and during hostilities assembled 4,700 Ansons and 700 Lancasters. At its wartime peak the Yeadon works employed 10,204 people.

The whole area was wrapped in a thick security blanket, as Elsie Stone remembered well:

"I was an aero fitter and became an inspector … We were kept away from the other workers and we even had our own canteen. The food we had was better than rations but we all did work very

left Airmen of 609 Squadron at Yeadon

above The CO's Hawker Hind (K6848) which pilot officer John Dundas crashed into a house on Victoria Avenue during the first pre-war formation take-off

left Gathering for a briefing at RAF Yeadon

hard. My sister worked in another area at Yeadon but neither of us ever discussed the jobs we were doing."

Muriel Kilvington Kay became an electrical wiring specialist working on the bomb doors and landing wheels of Lancasters:

"It was quite a change for me because before the war I worked in the Terry's Chocolate Factory in York. We were all

surprised at the sheer size of the Yeadon factory."

George Pilkington was sixteen years old when Yeadon was visited by Sir Roy Dobson, one of the main designers of the Lancaster:

"I was due to play cricket after my shift and was carrying my bat. He grabbed hold of my bat and told me that he was a Yorkshire lad himself and asked who

I played for. He spoke of Rhodes, Hutton, Sutcliffe and others and hoped that he would see my name in the Yorkshire team when the war was over. Long after Mr Dobson had gone, the people who worked with me were convinced that he was my mate."

I now have some German friends and we often compare notes about the war. When I told them about George Pilkington's meeting with Sir Roy Dobson, one of the Germans commented:

"That's two of the reasons why you won the war – your humour and the fact that the workers could actually talk to the bosses. There was another reason as well: we never employed women in the war and you did. Very clever that was."

top *The Lancaster Bomber Avro Yeadon factory*

above left *Elsie Nichols*   above *Sir Roy Dobson*   above right *Women at work at Avro Yeadon*

right *Muriel Kilvington Kay*

Yorkshire's Second World War airfields

There were RAF stations based all over Yorkshire, and each of these needs to be carefully and separately documented. It is not just the crews who lost their lives who need to be remembered, but so do the aircraft which were in the thick of the action.

Construction of **RAF Burn** began in 1941 and it opened in 1942 as part of Bomber Command. It was used by both British and Canadian airmen. In 1944 one of Burn's pilots, P/O Cyril Barton, was posthumously awarded the Victoria Cross for bringing back his badly damaged Halifax after a raid on Nuremburg. The station closed in 1946.

Catterick has become famous as an army camp but during the war RAF 219

above A Halifax bomber from RAF Pocklington on its way to a daylight bombing raid over Germany in 1944

Squadron was based there, as Terry Clark remembers very well. Terry joined as an air gunner flying in Blenheim bombers and was recruited before the war from an Auxiliary Air Force Squadron. He remembers that until he actually flew over Germany he had never fired a gun.

"We always understood that this was because ammunition was too expensive for us to be allowed to use it in training."

RAF Church Fenton opened in 1937 as a grass airfield operated by Gloster Gladiators and Gloster Gauntlets. During the war the station operated both Spitfires and Hurricanes. Flight Lieutenant J B Nicholson, flying from Church Fenton, was the only officer of Fighter Command to be awarded the Victoria Cross.

RAF Driffield opened in 1936 as a bomber station but with grass runways.

The station was raided by the Luftwaffe on 15th August 1940. They recorded 150 direct hits and did much damage, with twelve aircraft destroyed and several people killed. In 1942 the station was closed to allow the construction of runways to cope with the increasingly heavy bombers.

above Wrecked hangers and Whitley bombers of 102 Squadron, RAF Driffield, after an air raid in August 1940

RAF Leconfield opened in 1936 as a bomber station, but in 1939 was transferred to Fighter Command. At the height of the Battle of Britain, Leconfield was used as a

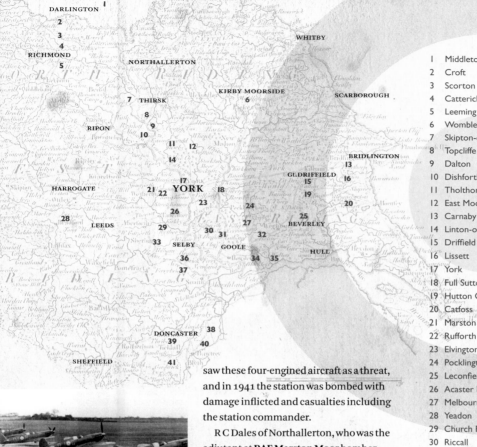

1	Middleton St George
2	Croft
3	Scorton
4	Catterick
5	Leeming
6	Wombleton
7	Skipton-on-Swale
8	Topcliffe
9	Dalton
10	Dishforth
11	Tholthorpe
12	East Moor
13	Carnaby
14	Linton-on-Ouse
15	Driffield
16	Lissett
17	York
18	Full Sutton
19	Hutton Cranswick
20	Catfoss
21	Marston Moor
22	Rufforth
23	Elvington
24	Pocklington
25	Leconfield
26	Acaster Malbis
27	Melbourne
28	Yeadon
29	Church Fenton
30	Riccall
31	Breighton
32	Holme-upon-Spalding Moor
33	Sherburn-in-Elmet
34	Bellasize
35	Brough
36	Burn
37	Snaith
38	Lindholme
39	Doncaster
40	Finningley
41	Firbeck

above Spitfires of 616 Squadron, RAF Leconfield

'rest' centre for pilots. It reopened as a bomber squadron in 1942.

RAF Linton-on-Ouse opened operationally in 1937. When Halifax bombers began flying from the station in 1940, the Luftwaffe saw these four-engined aircraft as a threat, and in 1941 the station was bombed with damage inflicted and casualties including the station commander.

R C Dales of Northallerton, who was the adjutant at **RAF Marston Moor** bomber station, wrote that

"the nights were long when they were on bombing raids, waiting to hear their return, counting them to see how many of them were missing … then there were two unhappy jobs. Next of kin had to be advised of fatalities … worse, the personal belongings had to be collected and sent home."

A royal visit to RAF Linton-on-Ouse in 1944

There were many nationalities fighting against the Germans, and none were so determined as the Poles. One Polish crew of RAF Marston Moor from a Wellington, which died on a routine training flight in 1943, have their own memorial thanks to Peter Whitaker and Jim Hartley. They traced the families of the men and some made a pilgrimage to the crash side near Skipton in 2007. Eighty-four-year-old Josephine Stebbing from Blackpool unveiled the memorial. She had married navigator instructor Jozef Wolnic just three weeks before the fatal crash.

RAF Pocklington only opened in 1941 but its Halifax bombers were used in support of the D-Day invasion forces; in 1945 it was transferred to Transport Command and operated Liberators.

There was an airfield at **Sherburn-in-Elmet** in the First World War, which was then neglected until taken over by Fighter Command in 1939. It was used as a satellite airfield by Church Fenton. By 1941, however, a decision was made to change the use of the airfield to aircraft production. Under license from the Blackburn Aircraft Company of Brough, it produced 1,700 Fairey Swordfish.

RAF Elvington is important for two main reasons. It is now the location of the Yorkshire Air Museum, but also it was the former home of RAF 77 Squadron which flew Handley Page four-engined bombers over Germany. This squadron alone lost 600 crew – more than any other single station.

In the early months of 1944, 77 Squadron moved to a new purpose-built airfield at **Full Sutton**, and Elvington was taken over by two French squadrons which were in existence until the end of the war. When the Frenchmen left in October 1945, Elvington became part of 40 Group Maintenance Command, and the airfield finally closed in March 1992.

Part of the old site is now occupied by the Yorkshire Air Museum. The museum is the focus of an Allied Forces Memorial which records the sacrifices made by the RAF 77 Squadron, the French 346 Guyené Squadron and the 347 Tunisie Squadron. There is a comprehensive collection of aircraft on show. There are also displays relating to a number of Yorkshire's aviation heroes including Sir George Cayley, Sir Barnes Wallis, Nevil Shute, Robert Blackburn and Amy Johnson. The museum is helping to ensure that a proud history can be continued.

Air Gunner Terry Clark

RAF Elvington

WAR AT SEA

MEN'S · ROYAL · NAVAL · SERVICE

the
Wrens

An unexpected invasion

By 1938 it was accepted by most British politicians that our islands would be invaded and that coastal areas all over Britain would be vulnerable. What was not expected was an invasion of quite a different sort. Once the people of Norway and Denmark realised that they would be overrun, many of their large ships, trawlers and small fishing vessels would risk the perilous journey across the North Sea and were determined to continue their fight from Britain. For many the trawler ports of Fleetwood, Grimsby and Hull were obviously largest and these ports became multi-cultural almost at a stroke.

Tomas Ericson's story is typical of many; he told me just before he died in 2007:

"I was working in the Copenhagen shipyard of Burnmeister and Wain, and I had only just qualified. We all knew that the Germans would march into our country and as I have Jewish ancestors it was obvious that I would face problems. A friend of mine was a fisherman and we set off in his small boat and aimed for England. Eventually we landed at Bridlington and reported to the authorities there. At first I was treated as a spy but they soon realised that I was a friendly Viking and I was
taken to Hull to work on trawlers some of which, like me, had crossed the North Sea from Denmark. I have never left Hull, married a local lady and hardly ever miss a Hull Kingston Rovers rugby match."

Many Norwegians also sought the safety of Britain, and played a vital role in the War of the Sea. Rolf Pietersen recalls:

"I was a good seaman and I knew the

North Sea very well. Hundreds of us look up at masts carrying the British flag but we also had pride in our own pennant which flew in defiance of the Germans. I'll never forget the welcome we were given by the people of Hull. I'm glad we send you a Christmas tree which decorates Trafalgar Square but I'd love to contribute to send one over the sea to Hull."*

above a Danish shipbuilder

below Tomas Ericson

Minesweepers

Before he became Prime Minister, Winston Churchill was appointed the First Lord of the Admiralty. He soon launched Operation Fish, to recruit vessels to perform the vital role of minesweeping.

Trawlers were ideal for this purpose, since they were largely built of wood and would therefore be less likely to detonate German mines which were fitted with sophisticated magnetic fuses. Despite this, minesweeping was still a hazardous job and many vessels along with their brave crews were lost.

The trawlermen were a tough bunch, as all were merchant seamen. John Bowes spent the war serving in minesweepers and he pointed out that

"we were mad when we were being shot at without firing back. Later they sent us to the Mersey where we learnt to fire some antiquated Lewis guns."

This form of defence was welcomed because many of the U-boat captains did not want to waste a torpedo on a trawler but preferred to surface and sink it by gunfire.

right Eventually, but under a cloak of secrecy, trawlermen were trained to use a Lewis gun and at last could fight back

above *The* Westella H124

above *The* Northern Gem *on Arctic convoy duty*

During the war many historic vessels were pressed into service as minesweepers or escort vessels. Two of these were the *Windermere* and the *Domino* which were ex-whalers sailing out of Whitby and Hull. Very few purpose-built whalers were constructed after 1890 but the one exception was the *Sierra*. She was built in 1929 and proved to be ideal as a minesweeper.

It was, however, mainly trawlers which performed this heroic task. One such was the *Lady Lilian* which was launched and trialled in 1933. The *Northern Gem* also proved her worth and was used as an escort during the Arctic Convoys. Dougie Porter was on these convoys and he told me:

"*I was on a big merchant vessel on the way to and from Russia and, apart from the weather, we always felt to be under attack. The trawlers were a real comfort to us because we knew that their crews were experts at getting people out of the water before they froze to death.*"

The Germans were well aware of the value of trawlers and did their best to sink them.

When a trawler was taken over by the Royal Navy, the Admiralty insisted that each was to be captained by a commissioned officer. These were nearly always young men, some of whom had never been to sea before and were often seasick. Ex-trawler skipper Derek Keetley put the record straight:

"*There was only one boss on the trawler and that was the skipper. The young naval officer was soon put in his place and usually only repeated the orders given to him by the old man of the sea – the skipper.*"

left and below Trawlers under attack

below left Trawlers and drifters from Fleetwood, Grimsby and Hull were requisitioned by the Admiralty

below right The Pentland Firth *sank off New York on 19th Sept 1942. This was the result of a collision*

be called upon. At the end of hostilities 60,000 men and 6,600 vessels were in service. Most of the men of the RNPS were trained at Lowestoft in a requisitioned municipal pleasure ground which soon became known as the Sparrow's Nest. The men were billeted with seaside land-ladies and referred to themselves as 'Harry Tate's Navy'."

Many trawlermen, including Hugh Evans, found themselves

"roped into the Sparrow's Nest and it were a good experience to feel that we were doing 'summat useful'."

Indeed they were: 243 trawler-type vessels were in action at Dunkirk and no fewer than 198 were under the orders of the RNPS. During the war 13,890 men of this under-rated service lost their lives. This represents a mortality rate of one in six. How well they deserve their memorial room at Fleetwood Museum in Lancashire.

Harry Tate's navy

When one looks at the annals relating to the Second World War at sea, there is an almost total concentration on the Royal Navy and the convoy systems. There are fewer accounts of the Merchant Navy, even less space devoted to the trawler-minesweepers, and the work done by the Royal Naval Patrol Service (RNPVs) is often overlooked. Charles Stewart has helped me to redress this imbalance:

"At the start of the war the RNPS consisted of skippers, mates and men of the Royal Naval Reserve, and initially there were 6,000 men and 600 vessels which could

Sailing into history

Kathleen Dabb of Scarborough has discovered that two local vessels played their full parts in the miracle of Dunkirk:

> "On 14th May 1940 the BBC made the following announcement: 'The Admiralty have made an order requesting all owners of self-propelled pleasure craft between 30 and 100 feet [9-31m] in length to send all particulars to the Admiralty within fourteen days'. The evacuation of Dunkirk, codenamed Operation Dynamo, took place between 26th May and 4th June 1940. Two small ships now well known to residents and visitors to Scarborough joined an armada of lots of little vessels sailing to Dunkirk to rescue thousands of troops trapped on the beaches. The evacuation was carried out by 222 naval craft and 665 civilian craft. The vessels succeeded in bringing back 224,585 British and 112,546 French and Belgian troops."

These two vessels deserve to be saluted each and every time they are seen or mentioned.

The *Oulton Belle*, now called the *Regal Lady*, was built in 1930 by Fellowes and Company of Great Yarmouth. After her exploits at Dunkirk she served as a fleet tender. One of her duties was to help in the transport of GIs from their troop ships such as the *Queen Mary* and *Queen Elizabeth* to shallower berths where they could be disembarked. Those saluting her in Scarborough should not fail to look out for the flag which is the Association of Dunkirk Little Ships.

The *Watchful*, now the *Coronia*, was also built in Great Yarmouth where my Uncle Albert was born. He worked in the yards at Fellowes and he told me:

> "I was an engineer by trade and worked on the pleasure steamer construction. Although they were built for gentle cruising they were pretty stable even in rough waters and we were always proud of the power of our engines."

Under her name of *Watchful* this vessel sailed to Dunkirk and back three times and brought back more than 900 troops. Visitors to Scarborough who enjoy a day cruise along the coast should remember that they are sailing in the wake of history.

left HMS Wensleydale *torpedo party, 1943*

above HMS Wensleydale *crew, September 1944*

below left HMS Wensleydale *at anchor*

Wensleydale at sea

It may seem strange that a warship should be named HMS *Wensleydale* after a Yorkshire dale, but this vessel has a short but proud history. Much of this vessel's story has been unravelled by Dave Allen.

HMS *Wensleydale* was launched in 1942 and was soon in the thick of the action. She was named after a Yorkshire hunt of that name and so it was appropriate that she should go on the hunt for enemies of the sea.

Dave Allen has chronicled several of the conflicts involving the ship. One memorable incident was when

"The crew of a Sunderland flying boat came down in the Bay of Biscay. HMS Wensleydale *tracked them down and picked them up."*

In 1943 HMS *Wensleydale* was one of a flotilla of ships aiming to intercept Nazi vessels bound for Cherbourg. Dave notes:

"HMS Charybdis *was the leader but she was sunk. Ernie Moseley told me he saw a sailor covered in oil ... He was desperate to get out of the sea but his oily hands kept slipping on the rope. So Ernie tied a bucket on a rope and pulled him out with that. Ernie went to a* Charybdis *reunion and told the story – and a man came and said 'That was me'. The two became friends."*

HMS *Wensleydale* survived almost to the end of the war and her demise came not in action but as the result of an accident. The vessel was at anchor just off Southend on the night of 20th-21st November 1944 when she was struck by a huge tank-landing ship. She was towed to Hartlepool and in 1947 she was broken up for scrap.

Yorkshire's little Kitty

In 1983 I had the good fortune to interview a most remarkable man called Charles Ayre, whose exploits just before and during the war around Hull Docks were memorable. His little ship was called the *Kitty*. The advantage of the *Kitty* was that she was small enough to get into all of the nooks and crannies and creeks around the Humber. Charles told me:

> "*Kitty* and me were much in demand [in the 1930s] by so-called German 'tourists'. If I knew now what they were up to then, I would have dumped the buggers in the water."

During the war Charles and *Kitty* were able to do much more useful work. At this time many trawlers were being converted into minesweepers and the docks at Hull were to say the least congested. The demand for experienced pilots who could manoeuvre among the berths was overwhelming, as Charles told me:

> "I was employed in the DEMS scheme which meant Defensively Equipped Merchant Ships. Seamen were ferried out to a vessel on which anti-aircraft or anti-submarine guns were fitted.
>
> "Another of my jobs, which I did not like much, was to cruise around the estuary and its approaches looking out for mines, plotting their position after negotiating round them. I thanked God that Kitty was such an easy boat to steer."

left Charles Ayre on the Kitty

below The Kitty with her open bridge alongside the trawler Lord Hailsham

Yorkshire's Wrens

Joyce Openshaw, who had been a Wren officer in the war working on secret cyphers, once said to me:

"You should not forget … the work that the Wrens did during the war. I worked in a cosy and warm cypher office but there were lots of strong girls who did backbreaking work."

Danielle Watson, now living in Australia, told me:

"Both my grandmothers lived in Hull and their future husbands were trawlermen. They joined the Wrens and they worked on loading torpedoes into submarines.

"You would be surprised how many girls from Hull and East Yorkshire volunteered for the Wrens, but most of them had lots of seawater in their blood."

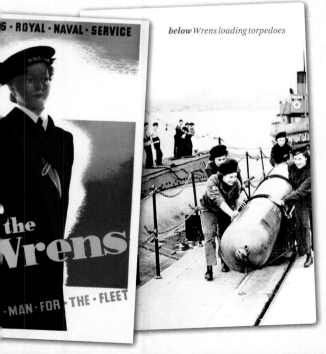

below Wrens loading torpedoes

Hull's trawlers go to war

"Four generations of my family had been shipbuilders,"

recalls Edith Heald,

"and they helped to construct trawlers for Hull. They worked at Goole and Selby on the River Ouse, and especially at Beverley on the River Hull. They were kept really busy during the war, not only because trawlers were being sunk during their use as minesweepers but also because the Admiralty commissioned what were known as Military Class Trawlers.

"I do remember HMS Coldstreamer which was launched at Beverley in 1943. She survived the war and reverted to use as a fishing vessel under the name of Dunsley Wyke."

right At the beginning of the war some trawlers were used as patrol ships

The saga of Convoy PQ17

Once the Arctic War against the U-boats ended, it is easy to assume that there were no mistakes made by those in command. This was not the case, and Convoy PQ17 is a prime example of the blunders which sometimes were made.

One of the vessels in that convoy was HMS *Bramble*, captained by Charles Lawson. His daughter, Joyce Openshaw, told me:

"My father was a perfect choice to command a ship in the Arctic Convoys because of his service in the First World War, during which time he fought in the Battle of Jutland. After the war he built up a fleet of trawlers which operated mainly out of Fleetwood but also had some vessels operating out of Hull during the war. When he was operating on the Arctic routes he was able to understand how important the supporting trawlers were."

In 1942, Convoy PQ17 set off for Russia. For some reason the Admiralty made a criminal error by signalling the Merchant Fleet to scatter and find their own way to Russia without the Royal Navy providing protection. No fewer than twenty-four merchant vessels were sunk and 153 men died in the Arctic waters. The Royal Navy did not suffer any damages or casualties.

Joyce Openshaw continued:

"When I talked after the war to trawlermen it was hard to imagine what it was like to operate in these waters without having the added threat of being bombed from above or torpedoed from below."

"LET US
O FORWARD
TOGETHER"

THE HOME FRONT

WOMEN OF BRITAIN
COME INTO
HE FACTORIES

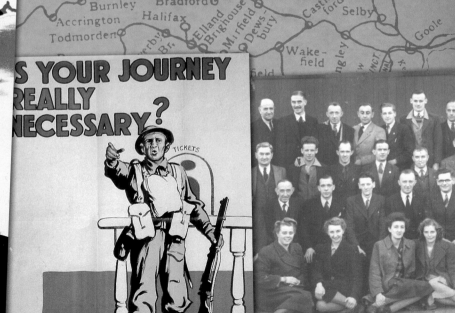

S YOUR JOURNEY
REALLY
NECESSARY?

TICKETS

Factory work

Like the rest of Britain, the whole of the county of Yorkshire soon became a massive war factory. It was not just local people who found work in the Yorkshire factories. They were joined by a number of 'off-cumdens', as Janet Pawson of Gargrave recalls:

"In 1939 ... my parents lived in Woolwich and dad worked at the Arsenal works there ... in 1940 ... my father who was Arthur Lampkin was transferred to a munitions factory at Steeton. He travelled on his motorbike and we later joined him and we lived in a small rented cottage in Albert Square, Silsden.

"Silsden celebrated VE Day with a street party around Windsor and Gloucester Avenue, and we all had a reet good knees-up.'

Obviously, Janet had by then picked up the Yorkshire twang.

Jacqueline Buksh recalled that her *"father had a cycle and toy shop in Keighley. During the war my mother looked after the shop and dad worked for the war effort at the National Switch Factory in the town. These switches were essential to allow electrical systems to function properly."*

The Germans had done their homework and some places were bombed not by accident, as has been suggested, but as a result of a planned factory attack which fell wide of its mark. On 1st September 1940 one bomb wrecked three semi-detached houses on Easterly Road in Gipton near Leeds. It seems likely that the raid was aimed at either the Blackburn Aircraft Factory at Roundhay or the Vickers Tank Factory at Barnbow, the latter having been an important ordnance works during both wars.

Arthur Lampkin with fellow munitions workers at Steeton

" LET US
GO FORWARD
TOGETHER "

Women in the factories

It was apparent to all that there would be a shortage of manpower in the factories. The solution was obvious: use womanpower. Women had already proved their worth during the first conflict, and in the second they were inspired by the poster 'Women of Britain – Come into the Factories'. They volunteered in droves.

One lady who had a most unusual job during the war was Elsie Buckinshaw:

> "I started work as an eighteen year old at Baker and Bessemers steel works in Kilnhurst near Rotherham on January 13th 1942 ... I was given a boiler suit and a bib and brace overall and lace-up boots ... I was escorted to my job as an outdoor crane driver ... The crane was situated outside the axle forge where axles for railway wagons were forged from ingots ... the axles were taken five at a time and my crane lifted them into railway wagons and off they went to be fitted."

It is likely that the axles went to the Doncaster works, and this stresses the importance of the railway network during the war.

Harold Benson remembers his mother-in-law who was only 4 feet 10 inches tall

> "but as tough as nails, she could swear like a trooper and smoked Capstan full-strength fags. She worked at the Fairburn Lanson Combe Barbel Factory. Her job was to bore gun barrels. At first some men thought that the women would not be able to cope. One big fat chap poked fun at our little lady, who promptly punched him just where it hurt and the two were friends ever after."

The women in the factories won two battles: one against the Germans and the other against male chauvinists.

Women at work boring gun barrels at Fairbairn Lanson Combe Barbour Limited

'Is your journey really necessary?'

By 1939 there were notices everywhere asking 'Is your journey really necessary?'. Soon there were fewer trains available because of the demands of the war effort.

Alan Hobbs of Sheffield told me:

"I was working in a Sheffield steel foundry and at weekends all I wanted to do was to get away from the heat and relax in the fresh cooler air of the Yorkshire Dales and coast … Instead I contented myself by writing down all the places I had enjoyed before things became disrupted."

Bill Donley worked as a signalman both in Leeds and at Dent on the Settle-Carlisle line; there he met and married a local girl called Rene Middleton. These days this line is regarded as just a tourist attraction, but when Bill Donley was there in the 1940s the route was of vital importance. But why? Bill Donley told me:

"We had to keep on our toes just in case

either the West Coast or the East Coast routes were blocked by enemy action or accident. The Settle-Carlisle linked the two and so traffic could be quickly diverted. The route passes through some of the most beautiful countryside in Britain and the summers there were idyllic. But I will never forget the winters of 1940 and 1941 and I have never seen snow like it …

"I'll bet people don't realise but we had to keep the blocked lines a secret so that the Luftwaffe did not know how many trains were stuck in the snow and presented sitting targets. I was stuck for days in my signal box, but I was warm by the stove and felt sorry for the teams trying to clear the snow with spades."

It was not just the main lines which were essential to the war effort and even the smallest of branch lines had an important role. Keith Hall, who worked all of his life in limestone quarries, told me:

"People don't think about how much stone was needed to make cement. Blitzed towns and cities had to be repaired, and how do you do this without cement?"

Armaments at Doncaster

Far and away the most vital of all the transport systems operating during the war was the railway network. Just as in the First World War, the Doncaster works proved well capable of performing a dual role: as a railway plant, which was obvious; but also as an important armaments factory. Not only were locomotives and rolling stock constructed and repaired, but also produced were anti-tank carriages and anti-tank gun mountings, four-inch naval guns, Crompton anti-aircraft searchlights and the hulls of Valentine tanks. Some women became very skilled in assembling parts of the gliders which were used during the Normandy invasion.

Blackout restrictions were put in place by 3rd September 1939, but it was not bombs which created the major problem for the works. On 24th December 1940 a fire broke out in the main carriage shop and it was fortunate that the conflagration was contained.

Even before hostilities began, much of Britain's railway network was beginning to show signs of age but the system just had to be kept going. There was therefore great pressure on the Doncaster works. Had the Germans succeeded in putting the plant out of action, the result on the British war effort could have been catastrophic.

above left Women assembling glider parts

far left Bruce Woodcock (later the British heavyweight boxing champion) at work at the Doncaster works

left The aftermath of the fire in the carriage shop

On the roads

It was not only the railways which were under pressure during the war. Those who made, repaired or drove buses, trolley buses and trams also had their hands full.

Coach builders were not only asked to construct buses and other conventional vehicles but had to adapt to produce vehicles specially required for the war effort.

Harry Watson helped to build buses, and he was not called up as he was classified as an essential worker. From 1940 until 1946 he was also helping to build army vehicles, mobile printing units and canteens for the WVS which were fitted with storage cupboards, a sink and a huge urn for boiling water.

Harry worked for Charles H Roe at Crossgates in Leeds. The parent factory was housed in two aerodrome sheds but in the end the aerodrome was not built and Charles H Roe took the units over. The quality of their buses soon became known country-wide. The firm built the bodies on top of chassis constructed by British Leyland, a huge firm based in the Lancashire town of the same name.

During the war the factory also made army vehicles and battery starters for aircraft flown by the RAF. This is yet another example of how every inch of factory space was used, and most factories produced a variety of essential items to help in the war effort.

Mobile canteen

Trams and trolley buses

Anyone looking at photographs of the bomb damage inflicted on Yorkshire towns and cities, especially Sheffield and Hull, cannot fail to notice the wrecks of buses, trolley buses and trams which littered the streets. Ben Crawshaw had firsthand experience of this:

"I was a tram driver in Sheffield. Some of my mates were killed, and the heat from the fires was bad that tram lines buckled and the tyres of the buses melted so that drivers had to get out of the carnage by driving on the wheel rims.

"I loved driving trams but even in the blackout we had to keep a wary eye open for daft pedestrians. They did not seem to realise that trams can't swerve."

Triumph motorcycles in full production in 1943

Motorcycles

In both wars but especially in the second, motorcycles played a vital role and were employed in maintaining fast communication links. They were potentially quicker and more manoeuvrable than four-wheeled vehicles, and were made in huge numbers.

Margaret Dennison told me:
"My father had worked for Scotts Company in Bradford but he was always ambitious and got a job at the Triumph works in Coventry. We continued to live in Queensbury but he got home on most weekends travelling on his Scott machine which he assembled himself ... He had been at home in Bradford with 'flu when Coventry was bombed and he lost many good friends. Until the day he died in 1987 he rode his 350cc Triumph which he described as his 'war horse'."

War on the waterways

These days we regard our canals as tourist treasures, but in the war they were an absolutely vital commercial transport corridor. A canal barge could pull enormous loads, and canals were by far the best way to move vital and heavy products. All the main Yorkshire canals and navigable rivers were kept busy transporting vital war materials. The wharves at places like Leeds, Skipton, Bradford, Castleford and Sheffield were as busy as a present-day mainline railway station.

Ailsa Buxton, who knew everything that there was to know about the canals of the north of England, told me:

> *"My grandfather, like me, had always lived on his barge. He was then too old to operate his own barge which was moored near to Bingley; he was asked to move it to a stretch of the Rochdale canal which was something of a backwater. He was given a very good radio, told how to use it, and a fishing rod. He was told to sit there and if the invasion started he was to report anything which he saw."*

Alan Bowes recalls:

> *"I were working on the canals near Castleford. Our job was to load coal from the chutes into wagons. We then pulled a long chain of these wagons to where the fuel was needed. We called the barges 'Tom Puddings' because of their shape when loaded with coal."*

Leeds-born John Pooley remarks that *"my father told me that the Leeds-Liverpool Canal and the Aire-Calder Navigation were always busy during the war, and folk these days don't realise just how important these canals were."*

Wartime winters

The winters of the 1940s were among the coldest of the century and there were also heavy snowfalls. Children love snow, and these days were remembered by John Murray of Holmfirth:

"It always seemed cold in wartime winters. We had moved in 1940 when I was nine years old from Cottingham near Hull to Grassington in Wharfedale ... the snow blew into the loft through gaps between the slates. My bedroom was in the loft ... and I quite liked the frost patterns on the windows."

The adults, however, saw these winters in quite a different light. Work was disrupted and transport – even the railways – often ground to a halt. The location of snowdrifts was kept secret; the view was that enemy bombers in moonlight could inflict serious damage on road and rail traffic.

The canals had a problem if the water froze but the engineers had anticipated this problem. Special boats called icebreakers had long operated. These had strong and sharp bows, and could be rocked from side to side by bargees who knew their business.

These days we worry about even the most moderate of snowfalls. During the war people were prepared to use spades, shovels and muscle-power in order to keep the traffic moving.

above John Murray sitting in a 'snow plane' with friend David Gunstone on the Green at Brooklyn in Grassington

above John Murray and sister Ruth in the yard at 5 Brooklyn in 1942

CLOTHING BO...
1943-44 General CB...
6

MEND AND
MAKE-DO
TO SAVE
BUYING NEW

MAKE-DO
AND MEND

ISSUED BY THE BOARD OF TRADE

...TCHEN WAS...

PIG FOOD

KEEP IT DRY, FREE FROM GLASS, BONES, METAL

DIG FOR
VICTORY

GRAND WAYS TO EKE OUT DATED OR WORN CLOTHES
Look Over Your Present Wardrobe; There Are Probably Many Ways of Re-making Old
Garments Which You Have Never Considered

MAKE-DO AND MEND

...e could do with thousands
...ore like you..'

...OIN THE
...OMEN'S LAND
ARMY

Rationing

These days we take supermarkets for granted, and you hear people complaining if they have to wait just a few minutes at the check-out; during the war, queuing was an accepted part of life. These days we eat what we want, but in the 1940s people ate what they were given – and that was not very much.

The authorities in Britain were well prepared and ration books were issued from October 1939, although the system was not started until the very cold January of 1940.

When you examine the meagre rations which were considered to be adequate, the amusing thing is just how healthy people were at this time. Before you go shopping next time, why don't you weigh out twelve ounces of sugar, four ounces of

butter, four ounces of bacon, two ounces of flour and one egg. Then add two sausages (meat was calculated by the quality of the meat; skilled cooks could produce excellent and tasty meals from what we now call offal). This was the ration for one person for one week. One thing is certain: fat people in those days were naturally plump and there was no danger of over-eating.

People could not save their rations – they had to be collected each week. The amounts allowed varied a little depending upon which supplies were available at the time.

Hazel Bayliffe recalls:

"My first real job was helping to sort out the ration books in Leeds, and this was not as easy as you might think. We first had to check forms to see who was eligible, where they lived and how old they were.

"There were ration books of different colours. A green book was issued to pregnant women and children under five. This meant that they could go to the front of the queue and were also to be given fruit if there was any available. They could also have two eggs each week and an extra pint of milk.

"Children between five and sixteen were given a blue ration book and could also have an extra pint of milk each week but only if supplies allowed.

"The rest of the population were given a buff-coloured ration book.

"All the books contained coupons which were cut out by the shop as the rations were issued. Each person was told which of the officially registered shops they had to use."

Barbara Middleton also had to follow the strict coupon routine when her first job was in a draper's shop in Halifax:

"*Everybody talks about food rationing but few people realise that the same rules applied to clothes. In this case, however, people were able to save up their clothes coupons but fashions had to change. Men's trousers were made without turn-ups, and ladies' skirts were devoid of pleats and no longer than just below the knee.*"

Treats were rare in those days but double rations were issued in Christmas week, and occasionally there was a surprise. This was certainly the case in Thirsk in 1943. A small consignment of bananas arrived in the town and was distributed to the children with a green ration book. The town had adopted HMS *Arctic Ranger* during a 'warship week' and the crew had obtained the bananas when they were operating out of Gibraltar. Marlene Jaques told me:

"*My mother had a draper's shop opposite a greengrocers. We had been told a delivery of bananas was due and I sat in her shop window all day waiting for these bananas to arrive. What a disappointment when they finally came, I didn't like them at all.*"

I remember my first contact with bananas in 1945, and for a while afterwards I was convinced that they were black and horrible as opposed to yellow and yummy.

above left Preparing the first ration books, Leeds, 1939

main image Strange fruit: bananas were a completely new experience for some

Taproom at the Hermit, Burley Woodhead

Cafés, canteens and community kitchens

Every effort was made to keep cafés open during the war, although careful checks were made to ensure that these were run in an honest manner.

Winnie Wenham (*née* Nicholson) was a waitress at the Blue Bird Café on the Grove in Ilkley:

> *"In the 1940s the Blue Bird was a popular meeting place for all ranks and was described by an army colonel as a cosy, home-like comfortable retreat."*

Some of the larger firms like Yeadon Aircraft Works had their own canteens, as the government realised that some people would be asked to work long hours and would need to be fed at work.

The government also realised that a few extra food outlets would be needed to supplement the rations. British Restaurants were set up by the Ministry of Food, run by local communities on a non-profit-making basis. (There was a huge purpose-built restaurant, which looked just like a giant Nissan hut, on Kirkstall Road in Leeds.) Meals were to cost no more than nine pence and no person could have more than one helping.

Fags and beer

They gave me this name like their nature
Compacted of laughter and tears,
Sweet that was born of the bitter
A joke that was born from the years

Their name! Let me hear it – the symbol
Of unpaid – unpayable debt.
For the men to whom I owed God's peace
I put off with a cigarette.

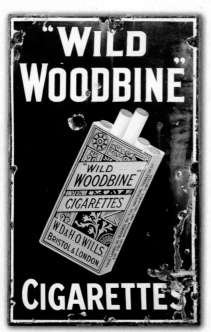

This poem was written by an army chaplain in the First World War. He was Geoffrey Ankatell Studdert Kennedy, the son of a Leeds vicar … and better known as 'Woodbine Willie'.

When you look at photographs taken in both world wars, almost every person seems to have a fag in their mouth. It has been said that an army marches on its stomach but was also true at that time to say that the whole country kept moving by 'fag power'.

When you consider that supplies of tobacco had to be imported, it is a miracle that supplies were sustained. What did happen was that smokers could never be sure that they would be able to get hold of their favourite brand. I remember my father queuing for two hours in the snow waiting for a supply of Senior Service to arrive.

Whilst not so addictive as tobacco, beer was an essential wartime weapon. Yorkshire was, and still is, blessed with excellent breweries. The worst thing that could happen was to go into a pub with no beer. Mike Comacho told me:

"I was an American GI on leave in Leeds
and I had just got used to drinking your
warm beer with a froth on top. One night
some of our guys were drinking and getting
on well with the locals. Then the beer
ran out and some of the locals told us
that 'We had supped too much'. Scuffles
broke out until another landlord diverted
us into his pub which still had supplies.
The booze had caused some ill-feeling
but peace was restored as the new supplies
came on tap and one of our guys got on
the piano and played Rule Britannia.*"*

Hazel Wheeler serving in the local shop

Dig for Victory

Dig! Dig! Dig! and your muscles will grow big,
Keep pushing the spade.
Don't mind the worms,
Just ignore the squirms,
And when your back aches laugh with glee,
And keep on diggin'
Till we give our foes a wiggin',
Dig! Dig! Dig! to Victory

The Dig for Victory campaign was not just an exercise to boost the morale of the people; it was essential to keep everybody fed. There is no doubt that it did work. Initiated in 1939, progress of the campaign was accelerated to such an extent that by 1943 it was estimated that over one million tons of vegetables were being produced in gardens and allotments.

Not everyone was honest enough to grow their own; some people raided allotments and sold their ill-gotten produce. Jim Allison of Leeds and others including Ian Grice of Barnsley recalled methods to deal with thieves prowling around the allotments, which involved the setting up of vigilante groups known as Garden Guards. By all accounts some of the toughest of the tough came out of the Barnsley coalmines who, as they put it, *"inflicted some damage on the intruders"*. Rosemary Nattriss began Digging for

Victory at the tender age of three. Her father was no gardener but in any case he was soon called up and so Mr Burnett, her next-door neighbour, operated both the gardens:

"He kept our two households supplied with fresh fruit and vegetable almost all the year round, and what we could not eat fresh, Mrs Burnett and my mother bottled and jammed for the winter months."

Mary Grant's family grew their own produce in wartime

At the government's request in 1940 the Women's Institute set up 5,800 so-called Preservation Centres to ensure that no food was wasted. It was estimated that just after the first Christmas of the war 1,600 tons of fruit had been preserved. By VE Day the impressive total of pickles, jams, fruits and vegetables had reached 12 million pounds!

The Ministry of Food was ever-active, producing posters including one which assured people that Doctor Carrot was 'the children's best friend'. Those who ate carrots would be able to see much better during the blackout.

If people did manage to take a holiday, the Ministry of Food advised them to go on to a Farming Holiday Camp and 'Lend a hand on the land'. One group which did this included Marilyn Neesom of Filey:

"It was the summer of 1945 and Grange Girls High School in Bradford arranged for a team of girls to help in the war effort. We were to travel to Wroot near Doncaster and were to stay in the Old Rectory, and we would spend two weeks in the fields thinning out beet plants ... we were paid nine shilling and sixpence."

Everybody was Digging for Victory, and in the end we achieved it.

The Land Army

Every acre of farmland had to be used during the war. There was the obvious shortage of young men as more and more were called up for military service. The country had to produce more and more food but with a potentially declining workforce. The answer was very simple: "Bring back the Women's Land Army".

The Land Army had been formed in 1917 and soon proved its worth at a time when Britain was importing much more food than it was producing at home. Despite this, the end of the war resulted in the old lessons not being learned and in 1939 we were still importing most of our food from the Continent.

By 1938 it was realised that there was going to be a problem with food, and the Women's Land Army was revived and

The war against mice

Land Army girl Mavis Horrobin (*née* Brown) engaged in a war not just against Hitler but also against mice:

> "I was sent to a hostel called Blois Hall at Sharow near Ripon ... we did every type of work; harvesting, haymaking, potato planting, picking and then sorting from a moving machine into bags."

> "The hostel was running wick with mice ... it was the usual practice when threshing to tie up the bottoms of our dungarees to keep the mice out ..."

> "Some of the time we spent snagging turnips actually on Dishforth Aerodrome. As we worked we counted the Halifax bombers returning in the morning and compared the number to the night before."

organised on a regional basis – in the case of Yorkshire, this was based on the three Ridings.

This process sounds so simple but it was far from easy, and a mountain of paperwork had to be produced to organise farmers and recruit the girls.

Thousands of girls from all walks of life were attracted by colourful recruitment posters and one of these was Audrey Bradley:

"I was working in a Bradford wool mill and it was a mucky job … I then saw a bill sticker putting up a poster on a wall in the Little Germany area of Bradford. This told us to join the fight against 'Big Germany' and so I applied to join the Women's Land Army. I had a reply from Mrs Harrison and filled in the forms along with my friend Doris Deakin and we were both accepted. We then got a bundle of stuff which included our uniform: rainproof mackintosh; khaki overall coat; two fawn shirts with a turn-down collar; pair of corduroy breeches; pair of dungarees; green knitted pullover; three pairs of fawn stockings; pair of heavy brown shoes; pair of rubber gumboots; brown felt hat; green armband with a crown on it; and a buttonhole badge which could be worn with civilian clothes."

right *Lady Bingley inspecting her Land Army girls*

'e could do with thousands more like you..'

IN THE WOMEN'S LAND ARMY

'Drinkings' during harvest at Lead Hall Farm, Sexton

Broadening horizons

Beryl Thorpe of Kirkheaton, like many others, found that the Land Army broadened her horizons.

"In 1945 and just seventeen I wanted to do something for my country ... and visited the services recruiting office in Huddersfield. I was told that being under eighteen my only choice was the Land Army. I expected to be sent somewhere in Yorkshire."

As it happened she was sent much further afield, and at Exeter Station she was collected and taken to a Land Girls hostel at Whimple.

"I was shown a list of jobs to choose from and I dearly wanted to be a driver, but being slight, I was dissuaded and chose to become a thatcher. I found it to be much more difficult than it looked and I was soon scratched and bleeding. I admitted defeat.

"I was then tested on milking cows and as I did have long fingers I was soon sitting comfortably on a three-legged stool."

Land Army memories

Although life was hard, most of those who spent time in the Land Army remember it with affection. For Freda McDonnell it was: *"A clean, healthy life, working on the land with plenty of fresh air and the companionship of other girls with lots of laughs …*

I lived and worked in Shipley. At eighteen if you were a fit woman … you were expected to either work at the munitions factory or join one of the women's forces … I joined the Women's Land Army … I expected to be billeted in a farmhouse … with an inglenook fireplace with a well-ordered farm kitchen with hams hanging from the ceiling. The reality was something else. We were billeted in a purpose-built hostel which was a low plain building in the village of Sawtry in Huntingdonshire, which was in a flat landscape with not a hill to be seen."

Mary Blackburn, then living in Hull, joined the Land Army and remembers capturing a dangerous spy – well, almost. She heard an aircraft in trouble and the pilot

left A threshing gang, August 1945

below A group of land girls at Whimple Land Girls' hostel in 1945

right Celia Little, a member of the Timber Corps

bailed out. The brave girls ran up to him armed with a pitchfork or a spade. The pilot could not speak a word of English but just kept smiling, which is not quite what you would expect from a Nazi spy. The local policeman was equally confused but soon a rescue squad arrived and then everybody smiled because the pilot was Polish.

Edith Thomas who was a Bradford lass until she joined the Land Army and worked near Linton-on-Ouse:

> "I helped with the harvests with pitchforks and later watched in wonder at the speed of the steam- and then the diesel-powered reapers and binders …Some of the tractors I worked with were real Heath-Robinson

affairs. One of my friends drove a Fordson tractor which dated back to the first war and another contraption I saw was a tractor adapted from an Austin Heavy saloon built in 1926. It worked well but that's what happened in 1940 – you had to make-do and mend."

above An early Fordson tractor

above right A Land Army troop with a Dales farmer

right The Mount Farmites

Make-do and Mend

It was essential that anything which could be of the slightest use in the war effort should be recycled and not be wasted. Iron railings were cut down and melted, and pots, pans and cooking utensils were collected and melted down. It has been suggested that much of the metal was of no practical use, but I don't think that this mattered because of the psychological boost provided when people were convinced that they were contributing towards the winning of the war.

These days we all live in a throw-away society, but in the war years people darned socks, and mended or unravelled old woollen garments.

Cups were produced without handles; the ballcocks in toilets had to be mended rather than replaced; and there wasn't even toilet paper – old newspaper was cut up, a hole punched in the corner, string threaded through and then hung up.

Smaller items in short supply included paper clips and gramophone needles. As a child my task was to keep the gramophone needles sharp and I was given a stern warning that, if I didn't do the task properly, George Formby would stop singing and Charles Penrose's Laughing Policeman would cease to laugh.

Special teams searched among the rubble of buildings damaged in the Blitz and what was not smashed beyond repair was recycled.

There was one unique piece of recycling. John Marshston, who was a Wellington bomb aimer, had been told to drop propaganda leaflets over Germany rather than bombs. Whilst on leave he had journeyed in his motorcycle and sidecar to his home in Hull. He had looked at the damage and saw a smashed men's urinal. He put it in his sidecar and on his next mission he dropped it over Germany. I'll bet those in Germany who recovered this present from the sky wondered what a Duckets urinal was doing in the Third Reich. This was recycling with a difference.

PALACE Theatre

FUN & ENTERTAINMENT

WEEK COMMENCING MONDAY, SEPTEMBER 14th, 19..
5.45 — TWICE NIGHTLY — 7.45

RUPERT

WITH
EXCITING

Keep on smiling

Everybody who lived through it knows that people did have fun during the war and, although they paid for their entertainment, there were also huge numbers of amateurs whose skills made life easier for those who just preferred to look and listen. There were sing-songs in the pubs and family gatherings around the piano, or the wind-up gramophone was a feature of Sundays and especially at Christmas.

The churches also played their part and in the winter Evensong was more like Afternoon Song in order to comply with black-out regulations.

Mildred Milner was a hard-working Land Army lass who made the maximum use of her spare time:

"I was stationed at the Royal Canadian Air force station at Linton-on-Ouse near York … money made from our produce went into funds which paid for entertainment on the airbase. Not only did I work as a Land Army girl but I also sang with a sixteen-piece dance band called the Linton Aires. The band also played at all the other airbases around North Yorkshire, plus Leeds Town Hall, Morley and Bradford, and we did Workers' Playtime from AVRO's aircraft factory at Yeadon which is now Leeds Bradford Airport."*

No doubt the Linton Aires took their name from the RAF dance band called the Squadronaires, which I remember from my own service days.

Workers' Playtime

This was an institution during the war, and must have been something of a logistical and technical problem at the time. All radio programmes were recorded live and the locations had to be kept secret. The announcer would say "Here we are somewhere in the North of England" or elsewhere throughout the country. Long after the programme was over, workers kept the event alive by providing their own 'playtime' sing-songs during meal breaks.

The gramophone

Alan Copley's memories must echo with those of others who wanted ready-made entertainment to sustain them in the war:

> "Saturday nights at my parents' baker's shop, 143 Old Leeds Bank … was different to every other night of the week … no baking was undertaken … only father was allowed to wind up the gramophone and place the loud or soft needle into the pick-up as the record specified."

A favourite artist of Alan's (and mine) was the tenor Richard Tauber, who was popular even if he had a German-sounding name. One of his songs was *English Rose* co-written by Edward German, who was British to the core and also wrote *Merrie England*. Songs like these kept Britain merry during the war.

main image Al Bowlly

Theatres and music halls

These days we regard a visit to the 'live' theatre as something of a luxury, but at the start of the war each city and town had at least one serious theatre as well as a live music hall.

When war was declared on Sunday 3rd September 1939, the Government made a decision – which in retrospect must have been a knee-jerk reaction – and which soon proved to be a major threat to the morale of the country. They ordered that all theatres were to be closed. Thankfully the Government soon came to their senses and all forms of entertainment were to be actively encouraged. The result was that Yorkshire's theatres and music halls were once again overflowing with patrons.

Listening to the wireless

Tommy Handley

No programme lifted the whole nation's spirits more during the war than ITMA. The host Tommy Handley deserves his place in our wartime history, but we should not forget one man whose name is seldom, if ever mentioned. This is Ted Kavanagh. Who? Ted was the man who wrote the scripts. There was a third man involved and he was the most famous of them all: his name was Adolf Hitler. When people spoke of Hitler they often said "It's that man again" and hence we have ITMA.

After all these years people still remember Mrs Mopp, whose catchphrase was 'Can I do you now, sir?" Then there was Colonel Chinstrap the army boozer who called out "I don't mind if I do" at regular intervals, but my favourite was Fumf the Nazi spy, played by Jack Train.

ITMA was also famous for its acronyms such as TTFN (Ta-Ta For Now) and the Entertainments National Service Association – ENSA – which was soon adapted to 'Every Night Something Awful'.

The big screen

During the war, cinema audiences reached record levels and the films were a great morale booster. Many famous actors honed their skills at this time, including Jack Hawkins, Richard Attenborough, John Mills and Margaret Lockwood.

The year 1942 brought *Casablanca* starring Humphrey Bogart and Ingrid Bergman. I remember seeing this film as a child and amusing the family by telling them that I had seen Umperty Coalcart and a woman with a funny voice. Apparently I had less trouble with *Mrs Miniver*. The latter was a Hollywood portrayal of what it was like in the London Blitz. I remember my mother crying after coming out of our local cinema after watching *Mrs Miniver*. We later tucked into fish and chips, and had a laugh at what we had seen on the Pathé News. This told us that Germany had just had to ration potatoes. We knew then that we were winning, because Potato Pete was alive and well in Britain.

left *A bomb-damaged Odeon cinema*

above *Lesley Howard as Reginald Mitchell, designer of the Spitfire, in the 1942 film* The First of the the Few

Holidays

In a county such as Yorkshire there had always been areas of open countryside, and each town had at least one park which could be used as a place for relaxation.

Mavis Kimberley remembers her wartime holidays in the Yorkshire Dales: *"In 1940 and 1941 my dad managed to save enough petrol to go in our little Standard Eight and it took us all day to get there ... he must have known the road because with with the threat of invasion all the road signs had been removed ... We arrived in Ellingstring. My uncle Captain Ball had retired from the army so to supplement his pension they had bought the village shop and post office ... Babs was his pet whippet. Babs was the best rabbit catcher and on one day she caught eight. Some were packed up very*

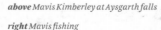

above Mavis Kimberley at Aysgarth falls

right Mavis fishing

carefully and sent off to friends in Lincoln. How grateful they were for this luxury ... We visited Masham, Middleham, Leyburn, Hawes and of course Aysgarth Falls where we paddled and took photos."

I was lucky enough to be a friend of the late Dame Thora Hird and she told me:

"I was a Morecambe lass but at times the town certainly earned the name 'Bradford-by-the-Sea'. My husband 'Scottie' had a dance band in the town and during the war there was usually a mix of armed forces and an occasional influx of holidaymakers, many from Yorkshire. Their numbers increased as the threat of invasion faded and the government appreciated that working folk were tired and needed some relaxation."

One unusual wartime holiday which I had never heard of before was recalled by Tony Taylor:

"My father who was an ex-soldier was encouraged to join the Territorial Army which he did ... he made everybody laugh by telling jokes in a thick Bradford accent ...my father's membership of the TA ensured that he had an annual holiday which was a luxury for people in our neighbourhood ... Each year there was a TA Camp at some place on the Yorkshire coast – Whitby, Scarborough or Bridlington ... The soldiers were allowed to take their families with them on these camps. They were put up either in large huts close to the men's tents or in local boarding houses."

above Mavis's family on holiday

Eddie Waring

Sport

The Rugby Football League minutes of August 1940 recorded the fact that

> *"The Ministry of Labour wishes it to be conveyed to this meeting that it deserves as much football to be played, so as to provide recreation and relaxation for the workers".*

At that time there was an intractable gulf between the fiercely amateur rugby union and the professional rugby league clubs. As the war started, however, there was an obvious shortage of fit young men, and movement became so restricted that players were allowed to turn out for their nearest club, be they amateur or professional.

In early 1940 a game between Batley and Hull was abandoned after sixty-five minutes as the air raid siren sounded and the crowd was directed to the nearest shelter. There was so much congestion that people may well have been at less risk if they had just stayed where they were.

In early 1939 the New Zealand Rugby League Tourists had arrived, but after only two matches it was obvious that the tour would have to be abandoned and the players transported home. In great secrecy the tour party were gathered together in Harrogate until a ship could be found to take them home. In the meantime the team wanted to do their bit to aid the war effort and proved to be world champions in the filling of sandbags. By mid-September they were aboard the Merchant Ship *Rangitica*, which evaded the attentions of the U-boat crews and other hazards during the six-week voyage. Once back in New Zealand, many of the team volunteered for the forces and

were soon packing down with the Germans in a much more lethal 'sport'.

One man above all others who kept the rugby league flag flying throughout the war was the Dewsbury journalist Eddie Waring, who managed the affairs of his home club during this time.

Eric Bowes remembers the importance of sport in the war years:

"I was nineteen and just back from being picked up off the Dunkirk beaches. I had a few days' leave and was watching a cricket match at Scarborough. I was sitting next to an old chap and I said that

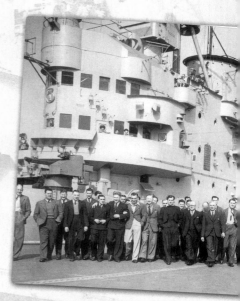

Rugby league tourist team on Indomitable *en route to Australia in 1946*

I envied those who had nowt to do but watch cricket. 'Aye lad,' he replied, 'I was in the trenches in the last war and being able to play English cricket is what we both fought for'. I have never forgotten that and it kept me going all through the war. As I heard shells exploding in North Africa I kept thinking about cricket and it kept me sane."

Whilst sport did continue during the war, it did interrupt and to some extent ruin the careers of many talented individuals including Yorkshire cricketers such as Len Hutton, Willie Watson and Hedley Verity, the latter being killed during the invasion of Sicily in 1943. Huddersfield lad Willie Watson, who played both football and cricket for England, was drafted into the army and played in teams alongside Tommy Lawton, Tom Finney, Joe Mercer and Matt Busby.

All sporting events during and just after the war were played in front of huge crowds, and provided with some respite from the tensions of work and worry.

Len Hutton

CRICKETERS, 1934

A SERIES OF 50
30
H. VERITY
(*Yorkshire and England*)

Hedley Verity, a slow left-hand bowler, first appeared for Yorkshire in 1930, and has since taken 532 wickets for his county at a cost of 12 runs each. In 1931 he dismissed the Warwickshire eleven for 36 runs and a year later captured all ten Notts wickets for 10 runs—an amazing performance considered

PLAYER'S CIGARETTES

H VERITY (YORKSHIRE)

Reading

My first hobby and one which has never left me is reading. I remember sitting in a cold Anderson shelter with the sound of bombs falling and reading by candle-light.

Comics during the war were almost legal tender to children, and back copies of *Dandy* and *Beano* could be 'bought' with marbles, sweets or bits of German shrapnel picked up during the aftermath of a bombing raid.

Apart from the newspapers which certainly left no room for escapism, what were adults reading during the war? There was a constant shortage of paper which resulted in libraries and secondhand bookshops always being busy. New books, however, were being published, many printed in America but copies did reach Britain.

Whilst working on the nostalgia of the war period I enjoyed discovering which were the most popular titles. The 1940 list included John Steinbecks's *The Grapes of Wrath*; the bestseller by far in 1941 was F Scott Fitzgerald's *The Last Tycoon*; in 1942 it was *Put out More Flags* by Evelyn Waugh which appealed to British readers; 1943 brought Graham Greene's *The Ministry of Fear* to the forefront; in 1944's bestseller list was H E Bates's *Fair Stood the Wind for France* (surely no title was more prophetic as the Normandy invasion was being planned); and in 1945, George Orwell's *Animal Farm* and *Brideshead Revisited* by Evelyn Waugh were bestsellers.

Mum helps with the reading at grandparents in Hull, circa 1944

Birthdays and Christmas

Listening to my mother and her sisters, the war to them was obviously a constant worry but most people were determined to shelter their children from what she described as the 'iron harvest' falling from the sky. Christmas and children's birthdays had to be very special days.

June Wardle remembers her Christmases when she lived in Hull. As a six year old she remembers how people got on with their lives even when they were enduring bombing. June's dad, home for a brief leave, made her a theatre out of a cardboard box, whilst her mum made the actors out of old bits of wood and wool. Her favourite present was the much-awaited Rupert annual.

I shared June Wardle's love for her Rupert annual, and I collected them from 1940 to 1946; my annuals were kept by my bedside in a little bookcase made for me by my Uncle Wilf, who also made me models of a Spitfire and an oil tanker which smelled of paint and which I kept polished.

Looking back at those days we can see how parents contrived to produce presents, as Marlene Jaques recalls:

"I was lucky that my mother and grandmother were competent needlewomen, and my father and grandfather were both handymen. I had home-made desk, chair, blackboard and doll's cot. My mother knit with left-over wool clothes for my dolls. Our dog even had a Christmas present. My father was a textile worker and when the picking sticks, which were made of leather, had lost their usefulness they made a very good chewing stick for the dog."

Christmas decorations were not a problem, according to June Wardle:

"We made our own Christmas trimmings, cutting lengths of red and white crepe paper. Tinsel was carefully preserved from one year to the next."

VE-DAY—IT'S ALL OVE

All quiet till 9 p.m.—then the London
crowds went mad in the West End

VICTORY!

VE Day & VJ Day

For those who did not live through the war, it is hard to understand the feeling of relief when it was all over. Even those who were children at the time only knew how to join in, but the sheer euphoria felt by the adults can only be imagined.

I can clearly remember the VE (Victory in Europe) Day celebrations but for me the VJ (Victory in Japan) night still literally burns in my memory. I was woken up in the middle of the night, made to get dressed and go out into a flat area where a bonfire was burning brightly and everybody was singing *Keep the Home Fires*

main image A dummy Hitler awaits his fate in Briggate, Leeds

top right Clarkson girls on Morecambe Pier on VJ Day

above right Victory street party in Halifax

Burning. Some girls were trying to sing like Vera Lynn with *Bluebirds Over the White Cliffs of Dover*; while teenage lads were roaring out an untuneful rendition, knowing that nobody, not even the vicar or the teachers, would stop them:

"Hitler had only got one ball
Goering had two but rather small
Himmler was somewhat similar
But poor old 'Goeballs' had no balls at all"
Beer was carried from the local pub, and

some enterprising farmers had roasted hundreds of spuds which were thrown into the embers of the fire and those with 'asbestos' fingers could help themselves.

Later, more orchestrated events were organised, such as street parties, where many people opened tins of fruit bought before the war and kept for a rainy day. In the event these were used on the sunniest of days for a number of years. Nobody worried about sell-by dates then.

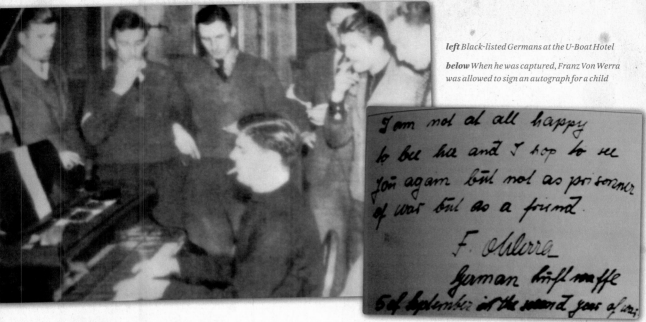

I am not at all happy to bee here and I hop to see you agam but not as prisoner of war but as a friend.

F. Werra

German Luftwaffe

6 of September in the second year of war

POW camps

I remember one of my old schoolmasters telling me:

> "I knew we were starting to win the war when they started to build more prisoner of war camps."

First came hundreds and then thousands of Italian POWs, but soon a trickle of Germans suddenly became a flood. The Italians did not present a security problem, but the Germans had to be individually interviewed and classified. The 'whites' were considered to be safe; the 'greys' were regarded as uncertain and had to be kept in more secure accommodation; then there were the 'blacks' who were Nazis to the core and had to be kept in very secure camps.

Most of the POW camps were low-key, as Margaret Merritt recalls:

> "We had a German POW camp down our road in Huddersfield. Part of the local park was fenced off and a few wood huts put up ... One Christmas a few of the POWs were allowed out of the camp to have a walk down the road. They always went back, so they were trusted and enjoyed quite a few outings."

Most of the POW camps all over Britain have long been forgotten, but Camp Number 83 can still be visited because it is now Eden Camp open-air museum.

Early in 1942, to the surprise of the local people, close to Malton on the road between

York and Scarborough an army sergeant arrived with a troop of strong men. They began to construct a barbed-wire enclosure, inside which were rows of tents.

The first prisoners to arrive were Italians captured during the conflict in North Africa. They had to help to construct much more substantial living accommodation made up of forty-five wood and concrete huts. The Italians were there from 1942 until that country surrendered in 1944. By that time Germans were arriving into the camp and many remained there as late as 1948. At its peak 1,500 men were held at Eden.

It was expected that all the POW camps would be dismantled after the war, but thankfully Eden had been retained thanks to the ambition and foresight of one man: Stan Johnson. His aim in 1986 was to restore 35 of the original 45 huts. The project has turned out so well that Eden Camp is now the country's most comprehensive museum relating to the Second World War. In each of the huts are displays concerned with rationing, Home Guard, the Blitz, the Land Army, Women at War, Dig for Victory, Make-do and Mend and many more wartime subjects.

But Eden Camp is more of a 'hands-on' theme park as my grandson recalled on his first visit:

> "It isn't just the things you see, there are lots of sounds, and I will always remember the smell which they have recreated in some of the huts including the one about the Blitz. This place is much better than the war games which you can buy today."

above Eden prisoner of war camp in the late '40s. The low white wooden picket fence in the centre of the photo was the demarcation line between the prisoners' compound and the British part of the camp

right Eden Camp today with reconstructions and re-enactors

Demob

What a relief it must have been when people left the services and went back to Civvy Street. Problems there must have been, but anything is better than being shot at. When they left the services, men were given the 'full monty' which was nothing to do with either a Field Marshal or a huge breakfast. It actually had a Yorkshire connection because those who left exchanged their uniform for a full suit of clothes. These suits were made by the Leeds company of Montague Burton – hence the full monty. Many of those going home were confronted by blitzed homes and were looking for accommodation.

Returning home

From the start of the war it was obvious that as a result of bombing there would be a housing shortage. Obviously nothing of any significance could be done until the end of the war when the demand for munitions diminished.

In 1944 the Housing Temporary Accommodation Act was passed. The houses became known as 'prefabs' and were designed to have a maximum floor space of 635 square feet (58.5m2). In the end only 156,623 were built and offered for rent.

The comedian 'Cheerful' Charlie Chester came up with this much-loved ditty:

Down in the jungle
Living in a tent
Better than a prefab –
No rent!

Each of the 'prefabs' had a back-to-back kitchen, behind which was a bathroom, which cut down the cost of long lengths of piping. The coal fire had a back boiler which provided constant hot water. This was at a time when most people did not have either a flush toilet or hot and cold running water. There was a built-in oven, Baxi water heater and a refrigerator – which most people at the time had never heard of.

There were many prefab designs, but

two of the most successful were produced in Yorkshire.

There was the Airey, developed by the Leeds construction magnate Sir Edwin Airey, who used prefabricated concrete columns reinforced by tubing made from the recycled frames of military vehicles. Although they were only supposed to last for ten years, many are still in use to this day. There are examples on the outskirts of Todmorden which are single storey, but at Harthill in South Yorkshire there are some two-storey structures. The Airey houses proved to be very popular and adaptable and 25,567 were built.

The Tarran houses were designed by the Hull-based building company of Robert Greenwood Tarran. His designs also included single- and two-storeyed dwellings with wooden frames and precast concrete panels; 19,014 of these were built.

Sir Edwin Airey

NATIONAL SERVICE ACTS, 1939-1941
Certificate of Registration

Assn. No. 475/3
Registration No. 6584

's Name CROSS Edmund Middleton Leeds

Address 87 Throstle Lane

of Birth 23.9/1924.

's Signature

READ THIS CAREFULLY

...re should be taken not to lose this Certificate, but in the event of loss, application for a
...be made to the nearest office of the Ministry of Labour and National Service.
...you change your address, etc., you must complete the appropriate space on the e...
...certificate and post it at once. A new Certificate of Registration will then be sent to...
...you voluntarily join H.M. Forces you should hand this certificate to the appropriate Service...
...You should not voluntarily give up your employment because you have been registered...
...ee.
...This certificate must be produced on request to a constable in uniform.
...A person who uses or lends this certificate or allows it to be used by any other pe...
...nt to deceive, renders himself liable to heavy penalties.

*M17527...
.S.2.

NATIONAL SERVICE ACTS.

ENLISTMENT NOTICE.

...TRY OF LABOUR AND NATIONAL SERVICE
...GIONAL LABOUR AND NATIONAL SERVICE, Regional Office,
...GATE HEAD,
WEST AVENUE,
ROUNDHAY, 20 AUG 1943 (Date)
LEEDS 8.

Mr. Edmund Cross,
87, Throstle Lane,
Middleton,
Leeds 10.

Registration No. LDT 6584

...with the National Service Acts, you are called upon for service in the
ROYAL NAVY
...present you... TUESDAY day 31 AUG 43 (date)
12 noon, or as soon as possible thereafter on that day, to
H.S. Pembroke,
R.N. Barracks,
Chatham

Latham (nearest railway station).

...Warrant for your journey is enclosed. Before starting your journey
...the warrant or a ticket at the booking office named on the warrant.
...ld be done a day or two before you are due to travel. If your warrant
...el from London you may obtain a railway ticket at, and travel from
... station to your address.
...a transferred on or after 1st June, 1940, beyond daily travelling distance
...r with the approval of the Ministry of Labour and National Service to
...portance, and you desire to travel home before you are required to
...u may apply for a free travelling warrant for this purpose. If you
...should on... immediately to the nearest Local Office of the Ministry of
... Service, and take the enclosed travelling...

...for 4s. in respect of advance of service pay, is also enclosed.
... receipt of this notice, you should, inform your employer of the date
... required to report for service.
Yours faithfully,

...for Regional Contro...

Registrat... Mr. Brian Whitley

NATIONAL SERVICE

Militia Men

To be strictly accurate, National Service ran from 1939 to 1963. On 27th April 1939 single men between twenty and twenty-two were called up for a period of six months. Initially they were called Militia Men and then they were placed on reserve.

As soon as war was declared, men between eighteen and forty-one were conscripted and they were to remain in service until they were no longer needed.

Even after the Second World War was over, Britain needed a military presence in many parts of the world. The National Service Act of 1948 came into force on 1st January 1949. All males between seventeen and twenty-one were required for eighteen months and were then placed on reserve for four years. The Korean War which began in 1950 resulted in the period being extended to two years, but the reserve period was reduced to only six months. The last call-up papers were delivered in late 1960 and the final National Serviceman left in May 1963.

Vital part of social history

Until I was asked to compile this book I had never written down my own National Service experiences. Once you get past a certain age it is hard to realise that you are yourself a vital part of social history. I hope that all National Servicemen who read this will be inspired to write down their own experiences.

In August 1956 I 'endured' basic training at RAF Wilmslow and then Halton before being posted to Malta. Like many other servicemen, between hectic periods of duty there was plenty of time for sport, leisure and sightseeing. From my home base at the RAF hospital at Luqa I planned a series of trips on a 1926 Harley Davidson motorcycle complete with sidecar; it was so noisy that the machine was affectionately known as 'the bomb.' I often visited Valetta with its bus station which was overlooked by the then NATO headquarters building; from there a gentle stroll led to Barraca Gardens which overlook the Grand Harbour, at that time full of British naval warships.

I still have friends on the island of Malta, and whilst I was there I corresponded with a pen-friend who has now been my wife for the last fifty years. I wonder how many other marriages came about as a result of National Service?

Along with my wife I returned to Malta in 2009 and 2010 on a nostalgic trip. We strolled along the margins of Melliha Bay and found a pillbox and a small concrete hut with a padlock on it. The building was our bathing hut, and the padlock on it had been mine!

above The author, during his National Service

The Grand Harbour - Malta

Square-bashing

All who did their National Service, whatever the 'mob' they were in, remembers their 'square-bashing'. I found it quite funny to be 'bullied' all the time but all that was being done was to lick raw recruits into physical and mental shape should they ever have to look after themselves in the event of a conflict.

Most people, myself included, tend to remember the jobs they did in the services and gloss over weeks of square-bashing. What nobody will ever forget is their service number, which is hardly surprising because you had to shout it out loud as you collected your pay. Mine was 5030533.

Neil Brittlebanks's number was 2585561 and he did his stint in the RAF:

"In November 1952 I was told to attend a medical examination at Templar House, Lady Lane, in Leeds …in late February 1953 I received a railway warrant which took me to Warrington and then on to Padgate to be kitted out. Then it was off again this time to Hednesford where we were drilled into shape for eight weeks … We were paid £1 8s (£1.40) per week; so we could not drown our sorrows too often in the NAAFI …After a few trips to the mess for our meals we noticed that the tea had a funny colour and an even funnier taste. We soon found out that the tea was laced with bromide, which [as a sedative] was supposed to dull our ardour."

KEEP THIS CARD SAFELY

NATIONAL SERVICE ACTS, 1939-1941
Certificate of Registration

Occ. Classn. No. 475/3   Registration No. 65846
Holder's Name CROSS Edmund
Home Address 87 Throstle Lane Middleton Leeds 10

Date of Birth 23. 9/1924.
Holder's Signature

READ THIS CAREFULLY

Care should be taken not to lose this Certificate, but in the event of loss, application for a duplicate should be made to the nearest office of the Ministry of Labour and National Service.

If you change your address, etc., you must complete the appropriate space on the other side of this certificate and post it at once. A new Certificate of Registration will then be sent to you.

If you voluntarily join H.M. Forces you should hand this certificate to the appropriate Service Officer. You should not voluntarily give up your employment because you have been registered for military service.

This certificate must be produced on request to a constable in uniform.

A person who uses or lends this certificate or allows it to be used by any other person with intent to deceive, renders himself liable to heavy penalties.

N.S.2.   *M17527 6/41 70

A driving force

Tom Porter, who worked as a chauffeur-handyman on several estates in Yorkshire, put his talents to good use:

"I did my National Service from 1955 to 1957 and I enjoyed every minute of it.

I did my basic training at Padgate, and as I was already an experienced driver I was easily placed and got a prize posting. This was to Jurby on the Isle of Man. I drove the staff car for Air Chief Marshall Sir Basil

Embrey. He had been shot down over France very early in the war and was captured but escaped and made his way back to England."

Widely travelled

Many National Servicemen were posted all over the world, such as Brian Whitley of Dewsbury, who served with the Royal Engineers between 1957 and 1959. He saw service in Cyprus, Suez and Bahrain.

"The normal age for National Service in 1957 was eighteen, but as I was an apprentice my period was deferred until I was twenty-one. In fact I got my call-up papers on my twenty-first birthday. As I was able to stand up without help I was passed medically fit, and I was soon in the Royal Engineers.

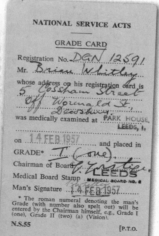

"I got used to being just a number but the experience was something of a mixed blessing. I was posted to various places overseas and learned to drive, but there was a downside to my time abroad. I had planned to be married but my period abroad put paid to that for a while. Instead of saying 'I do' I repeated '23386904' in order to collect my weekly pay.

"After a period in Cyprus at the time that EOKA was active, I was posted to places such as Suez, and a stop-off in Aden on the way to Nairobi and then to Bahrain. I remember that most places were hot – no, very hot – and full of flies."

I expect that most National Servicemen remember good times and bad, but many did see parts of the world, memories which will live with them for the rest of their lives.

A fitting posting

Tom Wilkinson spent his National Service on Malta from 1953 to 1955. For him there was hardly a break from civilian life:

"I was born in Skipton and had finished my apprenticeship at Rolls Royce in Barnoldswick. I was a fitter and worked on the Rolls Royce Griffin aero engines. I was excited to find myself posted to 38 Squadron RAF Luqa; this operated AVRO Shackletons which flew sorties over the Mediterranean to search for those illegally shipping arms.

"I was an engine fitter and it was really good to be servicing the Rolls Royce engines which I had been trained to assemble. You can tell how an engine is running by listening to it. You learn to pick up any alteration in sound.

"There was obviously a close relationship between ground and aircrew – the pilot has to be able to trust those of us in the service bay."

left *Leonard Firth (third from left, standing) during his National Service at the Royal Naval Hospital*

below *Leonard Firth (right) on reserve in 1954*

Mark Coleman's National Service in Suez; "Our first abode, a tent"; and "Lemonade (I hang my head in shame)"

A temporary stop-over

Mark Coleman of Rothwell near Leeds recalls:

"*In 1951 I joined the army to do my National Service and started working near Aldershot. I was a trained dental technician and this meant that I became a member of the Royal Army Dental Corps. In 1952 I was told that I was being posted to Korea and I boarded a flight from Stansted. The flight stopped off in Egypt, and the next morning I was told that the Suez area had no dental corps on service and they had decided to keep me there. I was there for almost two years, and I first lived in a tent and then in a Nissan hut.*

"*I have a photograph of me having a drink and I look boozed up but it was lemonade – honest!*"

In the navy

Not many National Servicemen were recruited into the navy but Jack Codman was an exception, and he enjoyed every minute of the period between 1946 and 1948. He visited Nice and Monte Carlo before spending time on Malta:

"Whilst in Monte Carlo the Prince had given orders that we were to be treated as his guests, and all bars and cafés were to charge us half the usual prices, and although we could see the effects of the shortages we were still able to enjoy the hospitality.

"A party of us were taken to the famous casino to be given a guided tour ... During our visit to the casino we were introduced to Moira Shearer and to Anton Walbrooke who were making the film The Red Shoes, *and were able to watch some of the scenes being shot on the steps of the casino.*

"I have also some other wonderful memories of our visit. One of the most outstanding ones is being in a bar very close to the

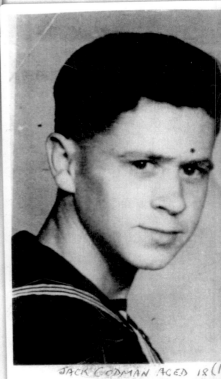

left Jack Codman and shipmate Len in a bar near Monte Carlo casino

above Jack Codman en route to Malta on the troopship HMS Corfu in 1947

JACK CODMAN AGED 18 (

casino one evening when the place was full of ratings from the American ship the Cheviot, and with many Foreign Legion members. Someone was playing the piano and a Legionnaire requested The White Cliffs of Dover which we all joined in to sing. An encore was called for again and again, but when a legionnaire called for the umpteenth encore an American sailor shouted that they had heard it enough times – instantly there was pandemonium when the Legionnaires en masse leapt up, overturning tables and started a free-for-all against the Americans. Seconds later the fighting spilled out onto the road and the whole area was like a scene from a western movie, the Brits were virtually bystanders as the Foreign Legion lads proved the truth of their reputation for toughness by outing the Americans in double-quick time, sending them running down the hill towards the harbour and the safety of their ship. Then almost as quickly, we all were ushered back into the bar by the Legionnaires where we reset the chairs and tables before resuming the drinking and singing. The Frenchmen had obviously enjoyed the episode and later in the week were again enjoying the company of the Yanks with no sign of animosity; it seems they just enjoyed the scrap.

"Most National Servicemen spent time in and around bars, and I was called to treat a bunch of sailors caught up in a fight in a Valetta club. As I was treating a young sailor I realised that I recognised him. He was Frank Park who had been a classmate of mine at school and was doing his National Service in the navy."

left Leonard Firth (back row second from left) doing his National Service navy training

above Two mates together in Monte Carlo

A sporting chance

Some National Servicemen who were good at sport had the time of their lives. One lucky lad was Dennis Birch, who served in the army between 1952 and 1954, and was about to be posted to Korea when he was selected to box for the army as a light-heavyweight. The team trained together, and the heavyweight was a young man called Henry Cooper.

In my own case I was training to play rugby for the RAF at Halton, and in the same gym was the boxer Dick MacTaggart who was the most famous amateur boxer of the 1950s. Professional cricketers like Fred Trueman were also much in demand for army teams, as were footballers and rugby players who were 'looked after' all through their National Service.

National service in the air

It was very unusual for RAF National Servicemen to be recruited into the aircrew. One exception, however, was Gordon Higgins of Ecclesfield, Sheffield.

In 1952–3 he trained as an air signaller, skilled in Morse code, radar, anti-submarine sonics, gunnery and navigation. He trained at Swanton Moreley for seven months, which explains why so few two-year men were selected; the RAF wanted regulars, to make it cost-effective in terms of both time and money spent.

Gordon Higgins (second left) at RAF training school

A royal visit

Selwyn Lockwood of Huddersfield remembers his RAF National Service between 1950 and 1952. During this time there was a royal visit to RAF Cranwell, where he was working in the post room:

"One day there were a few people standing round the noticeboard and we found out that Princess Elizabeth was coming to visit Cranwell. Everybody was very excited about this, including myself.

We found out later that a guard of honour would be required. I didn't know whether to be excited or terrified when I found out that I would be standing at attention with another eleven airmen waiting on the runway. We started training for the big day – what a shambles to start with. A sergeant came from the officer training section to get us up to scratch; it wasn't as bad as basic training but nearly.

"Then it was announced that the princess would not be coming by air as scheduled but will come by train, so a guard of honour would not be required. Crash went our hopes – all that square-bashing for nothing. "It was some consolation when we did get a chance to get a good view of her, and a wave from her. Within twelve months she was our queen. She did look lovely that day, as she always does."

A lovesick Selwyn Lockwood sent this photograph to his girlfriend

Acknowledgements

The author and publishers would like to acknowledge the help of the following people in compiling this book: Dave Allen, Jim Allison, Joe Arter, Ernest Astley, Charles Ayre, Esther Baker, Edwin Barnes, Hazel Bayliffe, Harold Benson, Doris Billington, Horace Birkin, Mary Blackburn, Alan Bowes, Eric Bowes, John Bowes, Audrey Bradley, Neil Brittlebank, Elsie Buckinshaw, Ailsa Buxton, Geoff Cain, Marie Caltieri, Glenda Chapples, John Chippendale, Terry Clark, Jack Codman, Mark Coleman, Edith Collins, Harry Collins, Alan Copley, Mike Comacho, Geoff Copeland, Ben Crawshaw, Kathleen Dabb, R C Dales, Emily Davies, Margaret Dennison, Ian Dewhirst, Doris Dickinson, Bill Donley, Tomas Ericson, Hugh Evans, Leonard Firth, Dennis Goode, Charles Green, Ian Grice, Billy Greenaway, Keith Hall, Olive Harwood, Roy Hattersley, Edith Heald, Gordon Higgins, Dame Thora Hird, Alan Hobbs, Mavis Horrobin, Edwina Jackson, Stanley Jamieson, Marlene Jaques, Derry Jones, Eric Jones, Derek Keetley, Muriel Kilvington Kay, Mavis Kimberley, Bob Kirkwood, Selwyn Lockwood, Rene Mackintosh, John Marshton, Margaret Merritt, Barbara Middleton, Mildred Milner, J Morrell, John Murray, Rosemary Nattriss, Marilyn Neesom, Joyce Openshaw, Laura Parkinson, Janet Pawson, Phil Penfold, Rolf Pieterson, George Pilkington, John Pooley, Douglas Porter, Tom Porter, M Robertson, Eric Shippin, Charles Stewart, Elsie Stone, Eileen Sykes, Alec Taylor, Tony Taylor, Edith Thomas, Beryl Thorpe, John Trelore, June Wardle, Danielle Watson, Harry Watson, Winnie Wenham, Brian Whitley, Tom Wilkinson, Dennis Woodrow, Dennis Woods, Gerald Woods.

Picture acknowledgements

609 (West Riding) Squadron Archives, p52 top left/right; Ackrill Media Group, p18 top/centre; Dave Allen (www.hmswensleydale.co.uk), p63; Joe Arter, p13 right; Horace Birkin, p46 left; Neil Brittlebank, pp114, 116; John Chippendale, p42 centre; Terry Clark, p56 right; Millie Clarkson, p108 top right; Jack Codman, pp120, 121 right; Mark Coleman, p119; Alan Copley, p97; Edmund Cross, p116 bottom; Kathleen Dabb, p62 right; Ian Dewhirst, pp17 centre, 20 bottom, 23 left; Clarrie East, p35 left; Eden Camp, p25 left/centre, 28 right, 43 right, 65 left, 69, 71 left, 89 left, 110; Eileen Donovan, pp91 left, 92 bottom right; by courtesy of Leeds Library and Information Services, p74; Leonard Firth, pp118, 121 left; David M Gowing, p23 right; Mary Grant, p87; Peter Green, p55 left; Nigel Hepper, p14 centre left; Gordon Higgins, p122; Kevin Hopkinson, p22 main; Hull History Centre (www.hullhistorycentre.org.uk), p36 left/centre; Marie Jaques, p4 left; Mavis Kimberley, pp100–101; Kath Lloyd, p4 right; John Murray, p78; Janet Pawson, p68; James Payne (www.throughtheireyes2.co.uk), p6 main; Jean Pedelty, p18 centre; Adrian Thompson/Lionel Marr, p59 left; Beryl Thorpe, pp90, 91 centre; Peter Wade, p108 right centre; Arthur Ward, p28 centre, 80; June Wardle, p105 left; David Watkins, pp13 left, 14 left/right/far right, 17 bottom left/bottom right/right, 18 right; Hazel Wheeler, p85; Brian Whitley, p117; Yorkshire Air Museum (www.yorkshireairmuseum.org), pp54 inset, 56 left; *Yorkshire Post*, p89 bottom right, p108 main.

All other illustrations are from the author's collection.